T0095351

Because of Love, He came ...

William H. Wetmore

WESTBOW°
PRESS
A DIVISION OF THOMAS NELSON
& ZONDERVAN

Scripture taken from the Holy Bible, NEW INTERNATIONAL VERSION®. Copyright © 1973, 1978, 1984 by Biblica, Inc. All rights reserved worldwide. Used by permission. NEW INTERNATIONAL VERSION® and NIV® are registered trademarks of Biblica, Inc. Use of either trademark for the offering of goods or services requires the prior written consent of Biblica US, Inc.

Revised Standard Version of the Bible, copyright ©1952 [2nd edition, 1971] by the Division of Christian Education of the National Council of the Churches of Christ in the United States of America. Used by permission. All rights reserved.

WestBow Press books may be ordered through booksellers or by contacting:

WestBow Press
A Division of Thomas Nelson & Zondervan
1663 Liberty Drive
Bloomington, IN 47403
www.westbowpress.com
1 (866) 928-1240

Because of the dynamic nature of the Internet, any web addresses or links contained in this book may have changed since publication and may no longer be valid. The views expressed in this work are solely those of the author and do not necessarily reflect the views of the publisher, and the publisher hereby disclaims any responsibility for them.

Any people depicted in stock imagery provided by Thinkstock are models, and such images are being used for illustrative purposes only. Certain stock imagery © Thinkstock.

ISBN: 978-1-4908-6644-4 (sc)
ISBN: 978-1-4908-6645-1 (hc)
ISBN: 978-1-4908-6643-7 (e)

Library of Congress Control Number: 2015900692

Printed in the United States of America.

WestBow Press rev. date: 1/22/2015

Contents

Part III. Epilogue

Preface

The gospel of Christ is the single most important message in the history of the world. There is no other message which contains the basic truths for the redemption and reconciliation of mankind with their Creator.

Mankind does not always acknowledge this truth, but that does not prevent this truth from being the truth.

Mankind cannot survive, to its highest potential, in the absence of the gospel.

At the heart of that gospel is both the Incarnation of Jesus Christ and His crucifixion.

His birth is one of the most significant moments in divine history because it sets the stage for the crucifixion, the resurrection, the ascension, and Christ's Second Coming.

Christ's Incarnation represents God's will to save repentant sinners.

I have always accepted the truth that Christ came into the world as the Suffering Servant to die for the sins of the world. That is of first importance; it will always remain so. God sent His Son to redeem and reconcile the world to Him.

For what I [Paul] received I passed on to you as of first importance: that Christ died for our sins according to the Scriptures, that he was buried, that he was raised on the third day according to the Scriptures. (1 Cor 15:3-4)

However, the Scriptures also identify many other reasons for His birth.

I believe that understanding these additional reasons will increase our understanding of God as well as our anticipation for the Second Coming of Christ.

It was the will of God that redemption and reconciliation would be through the birth, death, resurrection, and ascension of His only begotten Son. Jesus Christ, the Son of God, is the Perfect Sacrifice for the sins of the world.

Christ is also the perfect witness and example of the love of God; the perfect expression of that love is the cross.

Because of love, He came …

However, the Incarnation provides a multitude of additional truths that confirm the reality of God, the reality of the resurrection, and the reality of eternal life.

I have found this to be a most interesting journey, filled with many revelations of God's love, His will, and His purpose. This journey has explored many aspects of what the Scriptures tell us regarding the reasons for the Incarnation of Christ.

Our Christian life will be richer when the fullness of the Incarnation of Christ is more fully understood.

For that reason, I have written this book.

To God be the glory, great things He has done
William H. Wetmore

Part I. The Foundational Theology

Chapter 1. Introduction

And the angel said to them [shepherds], "Be not afraid; for behold, I bring you good news of a great joy which will come to all the people; for to you is born this day in the city of David a Savior, who is Christ the Lord." (Luke 2:10-11 RSV)

For God so loved the world that he gave his one and only Son, that whoever believes in him shall not perish but have eternal life. For God did not send his Son into the world to condemn the world, but to save the world through him. (John 3:16-17)

As we begin this discussion on the many reasons for the Incarnation of Jesus Christ, it is important to understand the background for the birth of Christ.

To begin with, there are several questions which demand our attention. Why did the Father send the Son into the world? What was the purpose? What was to be accomplished? What were the divine expectations? Was the world prepared to accept the Son? How would the world react to the coming of the Messiah, the Christ? These are only a few of the questions that we shall address in this book.

Also three doctrines present the foundational theology for the Incarnation. They are : 1. *The Love of God;* 2. *The Person of Jesus Christ;* 3. *The Cross of Christ.* These subjects will be discussed in the next three chapters.

The Scriptures reveal that God had an infinitely amazing plan for the restoration, redemption, and reconciliation of fallen mankind. He has at least 30 reasons for sending His Son to be the Lamb of God who would die for the sins of the world.

3

We shall examine each of these 30 reasons, for they provide Christians and non-Christians with an important vision of Christ, the reasons for His coming, the impact which God was destined to make, and the impact on the world which has had eternal consequences.

These 30 reasons for the Incarnation are presented in four groups: *1. To Serve God, 2. To Bring Salvation, 3. To Fulfill The Scriptures, and 4. To Transform The World.*

Now, in identifying these reasons, we must be quick to state that the emphasis for the Incarnation will always be as stated by the Apostle Paul in I Corinthians 15:3-4.

For what I [Paul] received I passed on to you as of first importance: that Christ died for our sins according to the Scriptures, that he was buried, that he was raised on the third day according to the Scriptures.

However, the other 29 reasons are invaluable additions to a more complete understanding of Christ's Incarnation.

Now, considering the 30 reasons, one truth is evident: the Incarnation verifies the reality of God, the reality of the Cross of Christ, the reality of the resurrection, and the reality of eternal life.

With this brief introduction, the passages at the beginning of this chapter set the tone for Christ's birth.

The first passage, Luke 2:10-11 RSV, is the proclamation to the shepherds which is the fulfillment of Old Testament prophecy and identifies Jesus as the Christ-child, born in Bethlehem, who is Savior and Lord.

The second passage, John 3:16-17, is one of the more beloved passages in the Scriptures. We need to *listen* carefully to all of the great truths that are contained here. *First,* God so loved the world that He gave His only begotten Son. He did not love without giving; He did not give without loving. With God, loving and giving are two sides of the same coin. *Second,* the reason God sent His Son was so that those who believed in Him would not perish but have everlasting life. God did not send His Son to condemn the world but to save the world. Christ came for justification, not for condemnation. As a result, there is no condemnation for those who are in Christ Jesus (Rom 8:1).

Here we have the foundation of redemption and reconciliation: Because God loved, He sent His Son.

Because of love, He came ...

The Incarnation of Jesus Christ, the Son of God, is that moment in divine history when God came in the flesh to redeem and reconcile that which was lost. He didn't redeem without reconciling fallen mankind to a loving, holy, just and gracious God.

The Son of God took on human flesh and added a physical dimension to His spiritual identity. As God is spirit (John 4:24), the Son of God is spirit. By the Incarnation, Christ is both fully man and fully God. Christ, as fully man, died on the cross and was resurrected. Christ, as fully God, is eternal.

Since the coming of Christ, the purpose of God is that heaven would come here on earth. That is what we pray.

Since the coming of Christ, the purpose of God is that there will be a New Heaven and a New Earth (Rev 21:1-2), under Christ, who is King of kings and Lord of lords.

Throughout divine history, Christ is the only foundation for salvation, which is redemption and reconciliation with God. (Acts 4:12)

Christ's Incarnation was necessary; His cross was necessary; His Second Coming is necessary.

This Incarnation was the only way that earth could become the image of heaven, in the same way that God's people can become in the image of their Creator.

Christ came from heaven to earth so that we would become the righteousness of God, that we would have peace with God and that redemption and reconciliation with God our Father would result.

God's purpose is that the Light, shown in the Incarnation, would penetrate the darkness and bring the lost into a relationship with the Light of the world.

We now address the multiple reasons for which Jesus Christ came into the world.

The chapters that follow will examine a broad range of reasons for the Incarnation: however, in this overall examination, we will find that there are both direct reasons and indirect reasons.

The direct reasons are based on the 12 statements in which Jesus Christ said: *I have come ...*

Do not think that I [Christ] have come to abolish the Law or the

Prophets; I have not come to abolish them but to fulfill them. (Matt 5:17 RSV)

Do not suppose that I have come to bring peace to the earth. I did not come to bring peace, but a sword. For I have come to turn 'a man against his father, a daughter against her mother, a daughter-in-law against her mother-in-law— a man's enemies will be the members of his own household.' (Matt 10:34-36)

Jesus replied, "Let us go somewhere else — to the nearby villages — so I can preach there also. That is why I have come." (Mark 1:38)

I have come to bring fire on the earth, and how I wish it were already kindled! (Luke 12:49)

I have come in my Father's name, and you do not accept me; but if someone else comes in his own name, you will accept him. (John 5:43 RSV)

For I have come down from heaven not to do my will but to do the will of him who sent me. (John 6:38 RSV)

Jesus said, "For judgment I have come into this world, so that the blind will see and those who see will become blind." (John 9:39)

The thief comes only to steal and kill and destroy; I have come that they may have life, and have it to the full. (John 10:10)

I have come into the world as a light, so that no one who believes in me should stay in darkness. (John 12:46)

Then I said, "Here I am — it is written about me in the scroll —'I have come to do your will, O God." (Heb 10:7)

In these passages, Christ said: *I have come* for the following reasons: to witness to God, the Father; to bring the message and means of salvation; to fulfill the Scriptures; to do the will of God, and to impact the world for the Kingdom of God.

In addition to these passages, the trial of Jesus Christ before Pilate, the Roman Procurator of Judea, adds an additional reason for His birth.

"You are a king, then!" said Pilate. Jesus answered, "You are right in saying I am a king. In fact, for this reason I was born, and for this I came into the world, to testify to the truth. Everyone on the side of truth listens to me." (John 18:37)

Christ, the King, came *to testify to the truth.* Since Christ is the Truth (John 14:6), in essence, Christ is witnessing to Himself and the purpose for which the Father sent the Son into the world.

To know the truth is to know Christ; to know Christ is to know the Truth.

However, the plan of God for redemption and reconciliation began with Abraham, to whom God first announced the gospel message (Gal 3:6-9), that through his *offspring* all the nations would be blessed (justified).

Your [Abraham] descendants will take possession of the cities of their enemies, and through your offspring [Jesus Christ] all nations on earth will be blessed, because you have obeyed me [God]. (Gen 22:17-18)

Consider Abraham: "He believed God, and it was credited to him as righteousness." Understand, then, that those who believe are children of Abraham. The Scripture foresaw that God would justify the Gentiles by faith, and announced the gospel in advance to Abraham: "All nations will be blessed through you." (Gal 3:6-9)

We shall see in the Scriptures the following progression: God's love leads to the gift of His Son as both the Perfect Sacrifice for sin as well as the Perfect Example for life. He, who knew no sin, became sin for us. Christ's death and resurrection leads to our transformation, to our redemption and reconciliation with God, and then to becoming a new creation. As transformed, we are to follow Him and make disciples of all nations. We are to be His witnesses in the world: we are to bring others into an eternal relationship with God.

So, understanding the many reasons that Jesus Christ came into the world will make us appreciate more fully the love of God for His children and for His Creation.

In addition, we shall see that these reasons show the seriousness of our sin and the tremendous love of God for His people.

We shall see how these reasons give us the basis for optimism regarding the Christian life.

We shall see how God is more fully revealed because of His love, His truth, and His peace which fill His Creation.

God is constantly reaching out to His people: yet, unfortunately, they do not always respond or return to Him. In the fourth chapter of the Book of Amos, God spoke of the sins of the nation and of the consequences of those sins. However, four times, God calls His people to repent and God said: *yet you have not returned to me (Amos 4:6, 8, 9, and 10).*

People ignore the need for God; people reject the love of God; people reject the blessings of God; people do not return to God, even when the reality of life shows the imperative for returning to the God who created them and loves them.

Throughout the Scriptures, we are encouraged to seek God. *If you seek him [God], he will be found by you, but if you forsake him, he will forsake you. (2 Chron 15:2)*

We are to seek Him and return to Him. That is what the Incarnation is all about.

With this introduction, we move to the foundational theology for the Incarnation of which the first subject is *The Love of God.*

Because of love, He came ... ...

*Because of **Love**, He came ...*

Chapter 2. The Love of God

The earth, O LORD, is full of thy steadfast love; (Ps 119:64 RSV)

A new commandment I [Christ] give to you, that you love one another; even as I have loved you, that you also love one another. By this all men will know that you are my disciples, if you have love for one another. (John 13:34-35 RSV)

By this we know love, that he [Christ] laid down his life for us; (1 John 3:16 RSV)

So we know and believe the love God has for us. God is love, and he who abides in love abides in God, and God abides in him. (1 John 4:16 RSV)

The love of God is the foundation for Creation, for all of the people, for all the nations, for all of history, and for every blessing in this world. From His love flows His truth and His peace: His love reflects His will.

The love of God is the central theme around which all of the other attributes of God revolve.

In many respects, the Bible is the story of the love of God played out over the ages.

As evidence of the love of God, consider the passages at the beginning of this chapter.

The first passage, Psalm 119:64 RSV, confirms that the earth is filled with God's love. God's love is higher and mightier than the heavens. God's earth and God's heavens express God's love.

The second passage, John 13:34-35 RSV, expresses the new command that Jesus Christ gave His disciples which is to love as Christ has loved us. Human love has now a divine perspective, and it is the evidence that we are Christ's disciples. Love defines our character and is measured by the love of Christ.

The third passage, 1 John 3:16 RSV, defines love, as well as gives the ultimate example of love. Love is the righteous laying down their lives for the unrighteous. The example is the Cross of Christ: the example is Christ Himself. The cross is the witness and love is defined by the cross.

The fourth passage, I John 4:16 RSV, is a fitting summary to the concept of love. The apostle John presents two truths about love. First, we know the love that God has for us; second, we rely upon that love for every thought and every act. We do this for the reason that *God is love*. If we want to understand love, then understand God; if we want to understand God, then understand love. If our life is a mirror of our love, then we live in God, and God lives in us.

God is the God of love (1 John 4:8); God is the God of truth (Psa 31:5); God is the God of peace (Heb 13:20).

God is the God of peace because God is love and His word expresses divine love. Peace defines our union with God. If we are one with God, then we know love, peace, and truth.

Although love is God's preeminent virtue, God is also a God of wrath.

His wrath is revealed from heaven against all godlessness and wickedness. He is a holy God who cannot and will not abide sin. The wrath of God is mentioned 197 times in the Scriptures, which the apostle Paul captured in Romans 1:18-20 RSV.

For the wrath of God is revealed from heaven against all ungodliness and wickedness of men who by their wickedness suppress the truth. For what can be known about God is plain to them, because God has shown it to them. Ever since the creation of the world his invisible nature, namely, his eternal power and deity, has been clearly perceived in the things that have been made. So they are without excuse; (Rom 1:18-20 RSV)

In addition, the Book of Revelation has 10 references to the wrath of God, closing with this passage in Revelation 19.

Then I [John] saw heaven opened, and behold, a white horse! He who sat upon it is called Faithful and True, and in righteousness he judges and makes war. His eyes are like a flame of fire, and on his head are many diadems; and he has a name inscribed which no one knows but himself. He is clad in a robe dipped in blood, and the name by which he is called is The Word of God. And the armies of heaven, arrayed in fine linen, white and pure, followed him on white horses. From his mouth issues a sharp sword with which to smite the nations, and he will rule them with a rod of iron; he will tread the wine press of the fury of the wrath of God the Almighty. On his robe and on his thigh he has a name inscribed, King of kings and Lord of lords. (Rev 19:11-16 RSV)

God's love is real; His wrath is real.

However, love is the divine keystone of God; it is the basis and foundation of His omnipotence, His omniscience, and His omnipresence. In addition, love is central to Jesus, the Christ. Further, the Holy Spirit is the Spirit of Truth who will lead us into all truth, which is the understanding of and the appreciation of the love of God.

Companion to love and wrath are law, grace, and truth. We shall consider the interaction of these terms as we proceed.

The Gospel of John addressed the relationship between the law, grace, and truth: *For the law was given through Moses; grace and truth came through Jesus Christ. (John 1:17 RSV)*

The law, given through Moses, was given to reveal sin.

But what is the grace and truth that came through Jesus Christ? What does grace and truth have to do with the Incarnation?

We begin by recognizing that love has two dimensions which are *grace* and *mercy.*

Grace is God *giving* us His love, which we do not deserve. *Mercy* is God *not* giving us what we do deserve which is His wrath.

Grace bestows love; mercy withholds wrath.

The ultimate evidence of the love of God is the Cross of Christ.

Now, love is intimately involved with grace and with truth.

Is love truth and is truth love? Yes, truth and love are inseparably connected. Where there is truth, there is love. Where there is love, there is truth. God is love; God is truth.

Recall the exchange between Jesus and Pontius Pilate. Just before being condemned to death, Jesus made this statement: *Everyone who is of the truth hears my voice. (John 18:37 RSV)*

Jesus came to testify to the truth. Since God is truth, Jesus came to testify concerning God.

Jesus also claimed that He was the truth. *Jesus said to him, "I am the way, and the truth, and the life; no one comes to the Father, but by me. (John 14:6 RSV)*

As God is love, so is the Son. As God is truth, so is the Son.

Regarding love, the Scriptures state that we are to obey the two great commandments which are statements of love.

Hear, O Israel: The LORD our God is one LORD; and you shall love the LORD your God with all your heart, and with all your soul, and with all your might. (Deut 6:4-5 RSV)

You shall not take vengeance or bear any grudge against the sons of your own people, but you shall love your neighbor as yourself: I am the LORD. (Lev 19:18 RSV)

We are to love the Lord our God; we are to love our neighbor.

As God loves us, we are to love God without limitations.

Also, we are to love our neighbor as we love ourselves.

Jesus Christ constantly emphasized the importance of these two commandments.

Divine love reflects the truth about God. God is truth; in one way that statement is the foundation that God is love. Because God is truth, we know that God is love.

Christ is the fullness of the truth: He is also the fullness of the Deity.

Christ witnessed to God by being the fullness of God and the image of the invisible God. (Col 1:15)

Jesus Christ said: if you have seen me, you have seen the Father (John 14:9). In Christ's great priestly prayer (John 17), Jesus prayed for the protection of His followers and confirmed that He and the Father are one: *so that they may be one as we are one. (John 17:11 RSV)*

There are many passages in the Scriptures which confirm that God is the God of truth. Not only is God the God of truth (Psa 31:5), everything coming from God is truth. Therefore, the Bible is the Book of truth (Dan 10:21); the truth of God will guide us to the dwelling place of God (Psa 43:3); Jerusalem, the holy city, is called the City of Truth (Zech 8:3); the truth from God is the basis of our freedom in Christ (John 8:31); the Holy Spirit who is the Spirit of Truth will lead believers into all truth (John 16:13); Jesus came into the world to testify to the truth (John 18:37); love rejoices in the truth (I Cor 13:6); the word of truth is the gospel of our salvation (Eph 1:13).

As evidence that God is Truth, consider the following passages.

Lead me in thy truth, and teach me, for thou art the God of my salvation; (Ps 25:5 RSV)

I the LORD speak the truth, I declare what is right. (Isa 45:19 RSV)

So that he who blesses himself in the land shall bless himself by the God of truth, and he who takes an oath in the land shall swear by the God of truth; (Isa 65:16 RSV)

This is what the LORD says: "I will return to Zion and dwell in Jerusalem. Then Jerusalem will be called the City of Truth, and the mountain of the LORD Almighty will be called the Holy Mountain." (Zech 8:3)

To the Jews who had believed him, Jesus said, "If you hold to my teaching, you are really my disciples. Then you will know the truth, and the truth will set you free." (John 8:31-32)

When the Spirit of truth comes, he will guide you into all the truth; for he will not speak on his own authority, but whatever he hears he will speak, and he will declare to you the things that are to come. (John 16:13-14 RSV)

Sanctify them in the truth; thy word is truth. (John 17:17 RSV)

In him you also, who have heard the word of truth, the gospel of your salvation, and have believed in him, were sealed with the promised Holy Spirit, which is the guarantee of our inheritance until we acquire possession of it, to the praise of his glory. (Eph 1:13-14 RSV)

God is love; God is truth; God is peace. Since the fullness of the deity is pleased to dwell within Jesus (Colossians 2:9), then it naturally follows that Jesus Christ is love, truth, and peace.

Christ gives us His peace. *Peace I [Christ] leave with you; my peace I give to you; not as the world gives do I give to you. Let not your hearts be troubled, neither let them be afraid. (John 14:27 RSV)*

Love is the evidence of truth; in like manner, truth is the evidence of love.

It is also true that grace, mercy, and truth are three different aspects of the love of God. Grace is love undeserved; mercy is love undeserved; truth is love. There is no greater truth than that God is love.

It follows then that love is central to the nature of every individual who would seek to be in the image of God and to lead a life pleasing to God.

From this discussion, it is clear that to define love is to define God. Such a definition is impossible for the human mind. I know that I cannot define God; in like manner, I know that I cannot define love.

The apostle Paul grappled with this issue. Paul said: I can describe love, but I can't define it. For that reason, we have Paul's great exposition of love in I Corinthians 13.

It would be presumptuous to claim to know fully the mind of God and the will of God. In like manner, it is equally presumptuous to claim to know and understand fully the love of God.

The Old Testament speaks to this issue.

Who has directed the Spirit of the LORD, or as his counselor has instructed him? Whom did he consult for his enlightenment, and who taught him the path of justice, and taught him knowledge, and showed him the way of understanding? (Isa 40:13-14 RSV)

Equally so, the New Testament speaks to this subject.

For who has known the mind of the Lord so as to instruct him? But we have the mind of Christ. (1 Cor 2:16 RSV)

No one can know fully the mind of God, the will of God, nor the love of God.

However, God has revealed His love in His Word and the fullness of His love is expressed in and through His Son. Therefore, God has given us revelations of His love which enables us to understand the character of love that God demonstrates and which He envisions for us.

The Cross of Christ most completely demonstrates the love of God. When we understand the cross, then we come close to understanding the love of God.

Two things I learn about the Cross of Jesus Christ; two truths come thundering in on me.

First, I am confronted with the seriousness of my sin; to realize that my sin requires God Himself to redeem so great a sinner. From the perspective of the cross, sin can never be taken lightly; the price of redemption and reconciliation is beyond comprehension.

Second, I experience *the enormity of the love of God.* How can a pure and holy and righteous and just God love me so much that He gave His only begotten Son that whosoever believed in Him would not perish but have eternal life?

The cross is a witness to the fact that, while we were yet sinners, Christ died for us.

He who does not love does not know God; for God is love (1 John 4:8 RSV). God is love: that is such a remarkable statement that no one will ever be able to comprehend it fully.

This brief statement might be the most powerful one in all of Scripture. Can anyone possibly understand the significance of these words: *God is love*? God, the Creator, Provider, Sustainer, Judge of all creation, is the God of love.

God loves you and me.

That is the basis of His creation; that is the basis of His relationship with His created; that is the basis of His promises; that is the basis of our redemption and reconciliation, achieved on the cross; that is the basis of the eternity which we are destined to share with God. That is love.

God and love are synonymous.

John 3:16 defines Christ's overall ministry and His primary purpose for coming into the world. Here we see expressed both the love and the gift of the Son of God. God loved, and He also gave. He did not love without giving, and His gift of His Son for the sins of the world is the most complete expression of His love for the world.

The love of God expressed in the Incarnation of Jesus Christ is that those who believed in Him shall not perish but have eternal life. God sent His Son into the world to save the world through Him. To accomplish that, Christ is the Light that came into the world, so that those who live in darkness would come into the Light. The love of God is evident and visible in every aspect of the life of Christ.

In addition, the love of God should be equally visible in every aspect of our lives. Because of that truth, Christians are called to be a witness to the love of God by the manner in which we love one another.

In this discussion, it is important to understand the results of God's love. Basically, we have peace with God (Rom 5:1) which is union with God. That is the same oneness that Christ spoke of in His priestly prayer (John 17). Further, we would have the Fruit of the Spirit (Galatians 5:22-23).

As love and truth are inseparable, so are love and peace. Peace is the product of love; love between God and man brings peace.

If divine peace were present in this world, the chaos and destructiveness of all people would cease.

There would be no sinful behavior such as identified in Romans 1:29-31 RSV: *They were filled with all manner of wickedness, evil, covetousness, malice. Full of envy, murder, strife, deceit, malignity, they are gossips, slanderers, haters of God, insolent, haughty, boastful, inventors of evil, disobedient to parents, foolish, faithless, heartless, ruthless.*

In addition, add to that litany, the wickedness identified in Galatians 5:19-21 RSV: *Now the works of the flesh are plain: fornication, impurity, licentiousness, idolatry, sorcery, enmity, strife, jealousy, anger, selfishness, dissension, party spirit, envy, drunkenness, carousing, and the like.*

However, consider some specific passages regarding the love of God and the peace of God.

Recall at the Incarnation, the shepherds were in the fields taking care of their sheep. *And in that region there were shepherds out in the field, keeping watch over their flock by night. And an angel of the Lord appeared to them, and the glory of the Lord shone around them, and they were filled with fear. And the angel said to them, "Be not afraid; for behold, I bring you good news of a great joy which will come to all the people; for to you is born this day in the city of David a Savior, who is Christ the Lord. And this will be a sign for you: you will find a babe wrapped in swaddling cloths and lying in a manger." And suddenly there was with the angel a multitude of the heavenly host praising God and saying, "Glory to God in the highest, and on earth peace among men with whom he is pleased!"* (Luke 2:8-14 RSV)

The announcement of the birth of Jesus Christ was accompanied by the great heavenly host praising God and pronouncing peace to all on whom God's favor rests. We can only experience this peace when

Jesus Christ is our Savior and Lord. His peace means redemption and reconciliation with God.

This is the peace which results from accepting the One proclaimed in Isaiah 9:6-7 RSV.

For to us a child is born, to us a son is given; and the government will be upon his shoulder, and his name will be called "Wonderful Counselor, Mighty God, Everlasting Father, Prince of Peace. Of the increase of his government and of peace there will be no end, upon the throne of David, and over his kingdom, to establish it, and to uphold it with justice and with righteousness from this time forth and for evermore. The zeal of the LORD of hosts will do this. (Isa 9:6-7 RSV)

The prophet Isaiah was told: *He will be called Prince of Peace.*

Consider Psalm 29:10-11 RSV. *The LORD sits enthroned over the flood; the LORD is enthroned as King forever. The LORD gives strength to his people; the LORD blesses his people with peace.*

Not only do we enjoy a life of peace here on earth; but, more importantly, we have peace with God.

As the Son and the Father are One (John 17), so are we one with God when His peace rules in our hearts. *Therefore, since we are justified by faith, we have peace with God through our Lord Jesus Christ. Through him we have obtained access to this grace in which we stand, and we rejoice in our hope of sharing the glory of God. (Rom 5:1 RSV)*

When we are justified through faith, we have peace with God.

When we have Christ as our Lord, we have peace because He is our peace.

For he is our peace, who has made us both one, and has broken down the dividing wall of hostility, by abolishing in his flesh the law of commandments and ordinances, that he might create in himself one new man in place of the two, so making peace, (Eph 2:14-16 RSV)

When Christ is our Lord, we will know the fullness of divine peace.

Peace I [Christ] leave with you; my peace I give to you; not as the world gives do I give to you. Let not your hearts be troubled, neither let them be afraid. (John 14:27 RSV)

When Christ is our Lord, we *see* His salvation.

When Christ is our Savior and Lord, we will know the fullness of love.

Finally, let us examine some of the passages in Scripture which express the divine love of God.

And the LORD descended in the cloud and stood with him there, and proclaimed the name of the LORD. The LORD passed before him, and proclaimed, "The LORD, the LORD, a God merciful and gracious, slow to anger, and abounding in steadfast love and faithfulness, keeping steadfast love for thousands, forgiving iniquity and transgression and sin, but who will by no means clear the guilty, visiting the iniquity of the fathers upon the children and the children's children, to the third and the fourth generation." (Ex 34:5-7 RSV)

O LORD, God of Israel, there is no God like thee, in heaven or on earth, keeping covenant and showing steadfast love to thy servants who walk before thee with all their heart; (2 Chron 6:14 RSV)

Surely goodness and mercy shall follow me all the days of my life; and I shall dwell in the house of the LORD forever. (Ps 23:6 RSV)

If you love me, you will keep my commandments. (John 14:15 RSV)

And hope does not disappoint us, because God's love has been poured into our hearts through the Holy Spirit which has been given to us. (Rom 5:5 RSV)

But God shows his love for us in that while we were yet sinners Christ died for us. (Rom 5:8 RSV)

We know that in everything God works for good with those who love him, who are called according to his purpose. (Rom 8:28 RSV)

Blessed is the man who endures trial, for when he has stood the test he will receive the crown of life which God has promised to those who love him. (James 1:12 RSV)

See what love the Father has given us, that we should be called children of God; and so we are. (1 John 3:1 RSV)

Little children, let us not love in word or speech but in deed and in truth. (1 John 3:18 RSV)

He who does not love does not know God; for God is love. In this the love of God was made manifest among us, that God sent his only Son into the world, so that we might live through him. In this is love, not that we loved God but that he loved us and sent his Son to be the expiation for our sins. Beloved, if God so loved us, we also ought to love one another. (1 John 4:8-11 RSV)

No man has ever seen God; if we love one another, God abides in us and his love is perfected in us. (1 John 4:12 RSV)

Romans 8:37-39 is one of the preeminent statements of the love of God.

No, in all these things we are more than conquerors through him who loved us. For I am sure that neither death, nor life, nor angels, nor principalities, nor things present, nor things to come, nor powers, nor height, nor depth, nor anything else in all creation, will be able to separate us from the love of God in Christ Jesus our Lord. (Rom 8:37-39 RSV)

I will close with this passage from I John 4:15-19 RSV.

Whoever confesses that Jesus is the Son of God, God abides in him, and he in God. So we know and believe the love God has for us. God is love, and he who abides in love abides in God, and God abides in him. In this is love perfected with us, that we may have confidence for the day of judgment, because as he is so are we in this world. There is no fear in love, but perfect love casts out fear. For fear has to do with punishment, and he who fears is not perfected in love. We love, because he first loved us. (1 John 4:15-19 RSV)

And so I conclude this chapter on *The Love of God.*

We now turn to the second part of our theological foundation which is the Person of Jesus Christ.

Because of Love, He came ...

Chapter 3. Jesus Christ: The Son of God

Salvation is found in no one else, for there is no other name [Jesus Christ] under heaven given to men by which we must be saved. (Acts 4:12)

God made him [Christ] who had no sin to be sin for us, so that in him we might become the righteousness of God. (2 Cor 5:21)

… that at the name of Jesus every knee should bow, in heaven and on earth and under the earth, and every tongue confess that Jesus Christ is Lord, to the glory of God the Father. (Phil 2:10-11)

He is the image of the invisible God (Col 1:15)

We now address the Person of Jesus Christ, the Son of God who is equally God the Son.

The four passages at the beginning of this chapter give us a glimpse of His Person.

The first passage, Acts 4:12, states that salvation is through Christ alone. Christ said: *no one comes to the Father, except through me. (John 14:6)*

The second passage, 2 Corinthians 5:21, states that, on the cross, Christ took on our sins and gave us His righteousness. This was the divine exchange of righteousness for sin that occurred on the cross.

The third passage, Philippians 2:10-11, states that God, the Father, has glorified His only begotten Son, so that every knee should bow and every tongue confess that Jesus Christ is Lord, to the glory of God the Father.

The fourth passage, Colossians 1:15, states that Jesus Christ is fully

God. The Son of God is God the Son. Many will acknowledge that Jesus Christ is the Son of God. Jesus Christ said: *If you have seen me, you have seen the Father.*

This brief summary gives us insight into the nature and character of Jesus Christ, the Son of God.

However, it is vital that we understand the Person of Jesus Christ; only then can we understand the Incarnation and the consequences that it has produced for all people and nations since His birth.

In addition, we must have a strong, committed, and abiding relationship with Him. We can only produce fruit in this life if *we abide in Him and He in us … for apart from Him we can do nothing. (John 15:5)*

The Son of God came to die for the sins of the world, to witness to the truth (John 18:37), and to give His righteousness to all who receive Him and believe in His name (John 1:12).

He is the Christ. He is the image of the invisible God. He is the Revelation of God. He is the Word made flesh; He is God Incarnate. He is the Suffering Servant. He is the child who is the mighty God, the Prince of Peace. He is the Alpha and the Omega. He is the Faithful One. He is the perfect Sacrifice. He is our Teacher. He is our Preacher. He is the Author of our salvation. He is the good Shepherd who lays down His life for the sheep. He is the Bread of life. He is the Light of the world. He is the Door for the sheep. He is the resurrection and the life. He is the Way, the Truth, and the Life. He is the True Vine. He is the Savior of the world. He is our great High Priest. He is the Head of the body, the church. He has all authority in heaven and on earth. He is King of kings and Lord of lords.

In all of these truths, the primary truth is that the Son of God is God the Son. This truth is critical to our understanding of Jesus Christ. Many acknowledge Christ as the Son of God but fail to acknowledge Christ as God.

For in Christ all the fullness of the Deity lives in bodily form, and you have been given fullness in Christ, who is the head over every power and authority. (Col 2:9-10)

He is fully God; He is fully man.

So, in the following five areas, let us examine this Messiah, this Christ, this Son of God, this Savior, this Lord of the world: *first,* as the image of the invisible God; *second*, as our Savior; *third, as* our Lord; *fourth*, as our eternal Teacher; *fifth*, as our Preacher.

First, Jesus Christ: the image of the invisible God

He is the image of the invisible God, the firstborn over all creation. For by him all things were created: things in heaven and on earth, visible and invisible, whether thrones or powers or rulers or authorities; all things were created by him and for him. He is before all things, and in him all things hold together. And he is the head of the body, the church; he is the beginning and the firstborn from among the dead, so that in everything he might have the supremacy. For God was pleased to have all his fullness dwell in him, and through him to reconcile to himself all things, whether things on earth or things in heaven, by making peace through his blood, shed on the cross. (Col 1:15-20)

There are a multiple of truths and revelations in this passage.

The first truth deals with the invisibility of God. The pagan nations had always confronted the Jews with the statement: you worship an invisible God. That was a problem for the Jews until the Incarnation, the coming of God in the flesh.

Then the Apostle John wrote: *No one has ever seen God, but God the One and Only, who is at the Father's side, has made him known. (John 1:18)*

So, with the coming of Christ, God is no longer invisible: God is now visible in His Son.

However, with the death, resurrection, and ascension of Christ, is God invisible again?

The apostle John addressed this subject, using the same formula.

No one has ever seen God; but if we love one another, God lives in us and his love is made complete in us. (1 John 4:12)

John said: *if we love one another, God lives in us and his love is made complete in us.*

Is God invisible now? No, God is now visible in His people and in His church, if we love one another. God is no longer invisible.

The second truth is that Jesus Christ, the Son of God, is the *firstborn over all creation.*

The third truth is that *by him all things were created: things in heaven* and on earth, visible and invisible, whether thrones or powers or rulers or authorities; all things were created by him and for him.

The fourth truth is that Jesus Christ *is before all things, and in him all things hold together.*

The fifth truth is that *he is the head of the body, the church.*

The sixth truth is that *he is the beginning and the firstborn from among the dead, so that in everything he might have the supremacy.*

The seventh truth is that *God was pleased to have all his fullness dwell in him, and through him to reconcile to himself all things, whether things on earth or things in heaven, by making peace through his blood, shed on the cross.*

All of these truths combine to define the Person of Jesus Christ, the Son of God.

Second, Jesus Christ: our Savior
In the Old Testament, God is rightly recognized as the Creator of the world and as the Savior of the nation, Israel.

Give thanks to the LORD, for he is good; his love endures forever. Cry out, "Save us, O God our Savior; gather us and deliver us from the nations, that we may give thanks to your holy name, that we may glory in your praise." (1 Chron 16:34-35)

He will call out to me, 'You are my Father, my God, the Rock my Savior.' (Ps 89:26)

As Christ is the image of the invisible God, it is natural that He would also be recognized as the Savior, not just of Israel, but as the Savior of the world. As God is Savior, so is Christ.

All nations will be blessed (justified) by Christ our Savior and our Lord, who is the offspring of Abraham. (Matt 1:1)

From this man's descendants [David] God has brought to Israel the Savior Jesus, as he promised. (Acts 13:23)

But our citizenship is in heaven. And we eagerly await a Savior from there, the Lord Jesus Christ, who, by the power that enables him to bring everything under his control, will transform our lowly bodies so that they will be like his glorious body. (Phil 3:20-21)

God has highly exalted His Son and given Him the name that is above every name, so, that at the name of Jesus every knee should bow, and every tongue should confess that Jesus Christ is Lord, to the glory of God the Father.

Jesus Christ came into the world to be the Savior of the world. Our Savior is also our Redeemer and our Advocate. (I John 2:1)

He saved us by at least two acts: first, He took on our sins; second, He gave us His righteousness so that we could become the children of God. He has opened the door of heaven so that we might receive the love of God.

As we honor Jesus Christ as Savior, we also honor Him as Lord. He is Savior and Lord; He is both. He cannot be one without being the other.

Third, Jesus Christ: our Lord

To recognize Jesus Christ as our Lord means that we accept Christ as God. He is the Son of God who is also God the Son.

He is fully God and fully man. He is the Source of our restored and renewed relationship with God the Father; He is the One through whom we have gained access to the love of God. He has redeemed us and reconciled us to our Creator. Such restoration means that we have peace with God, which means that, through Christ, we are one with the Father.

Therefore, since we have been justified through faith, we have peace with God through our Lord Jesus Christ, through whom we have gained access by faith into this grace in which we now stand. (Rom 5:1-2)

Through Jesus Christ, we have been saved from sin; we have gained the victory which can only come through faith in our Lord Jesus Christ.

The sting of death is sin, and the power of sin is the law. But thanks be to God! He gives us the victory through our Lord Jesus Christ. (1 Cor 15:56-57)

He was in the world, and though the world was made through him, the world did not recognize him. He came to that which was his own, but his own did not receive him. Yet to all who received him, to those who believed in his name, he gave the right to become children of God—children born not of natural descent, nor of human decision or a husband's will, but born of God. (John 1:10-13)

There are two essential affirmations that we must make if we are to have God as our Father and if we are to have Christ as our Savior and Lord. First, we must *receive* Him; second, we must *believe in his name.*

When we receive and believe in Christ as Savior and Lord, then we shall be born of God. Then we shall become a child of God. Then we can call God, our Father.

Fourth, Jesus Christ: our eternal Teacher

Throughout the New Testament, Jesus Christ is universally acknowledged as *Teacher,* by the Jewish teachers of the law (Matt 8:19), by the Pharisees (Matt 9:11), by tax collectors (Matt 17:24), by His disciples (Mk 4:38), by the rich man (Mk 10:17), by Peter (Luke 7:40), by the ruler of the synagogue (Luke 8:49), and by experts in the law (Luke 10:25).

However, Christ told His disciples that they are not to be called *teachers* for He alone is their Teacher (Matt 23:8).

Christians have one Savior, one Lord, one Perfect Sacrifice, and one Teacher, Jesus Christ.

Now, His teachings are in three distinct areas: 1. He taught with signs; 2. He taught with direct statements of His deity; 3. He taught in parables.

However, in the midst of His teachings, there are consistently the warnings of Scripture (e.g. Isaiah 6).

He [the Lord] said, "Go and tell this people: 'Be ever hearing, but never understanding; be ever seeing, but never perceiving. (Isa 6:9)

In Matthew 13:14-15, Jesus repeated this same message to the Israelites: the message of God then is the message to all the nations throughout history and especially today.

In all biblical teaching, people need to hear and to understand; people need to see and to perceive. The evidence of hearing is obedience; the evidence of seeing is to perceive the spiritual truth that is present in what is seen. So let us *see* the teachings of Christ.

Jesus taught with signs. Now, a sign points to or represents something larger or more important than itself, which represents the acts of God. Signs point primarily to the redeeming activity of God as experienced through the ministry of Jesus and the apostles.

Throughout the Bible, the significance of a sign is understood only through faith. Also signs are distinct from miracles, because signs point to the divine power which is evident in the event and to the supernatural power that makes the event possible. In addition, the sign shows the work of God or a unique revelation of God. Finally, the sign calls for a response in faith and obedience from those who witness the sign.

The Gospel of John identified the six signs of Christ:

- *The Wedding Feast in Cana (2:1-11)*
- *The Healing of the Son of an Official (4:46-54)*
- *The Healing of the Paralytic (5:1-21)*
- *The Feeding of the Five Thousand (6:1-14)*
- *The Healing of the Blind Man (9:1-25)*
- *The Raising of Lazarus (11:1-44)*

The Apostle John testified that Jesus did many other signs which are not recorded in this book. *Jesus did many other miraculous signs in the presence of his disciples, which are not recorded in this book. But these are written that you may believe that Jesus is the Christ, the Son of God, and that by believing you may have life in his name. (John 20:30-31)*

John said that the signs were given for two reasons: *first*, that we would believe that Jesus is the Christ, the Son of God; *second*, that, by *believing in Him*, we would have eternal life.

Let us examine briefly the six signs.

In *the Wedding Feast,* the *good wine* is His blood, shed for sinners, to provide for the forgiveness of sin and to redeem and rescue sinners from this evil age.

In *the Healing of the Son of an Official,* the importance of faith is verified.

In *the Healing of the Paralytic,* Jesus Christ explained that He has come for the helpless and to heal those of faith.

In *The Feeding of the Five Thousand,* the bread and the fish are a reminder of God's faithfulness and provision in *feeding* those who come to Him for salvation. Jesus said that He is the *true bread* that came down from heaven and gives *salvation (life)* to the world.

In *the Healing of the Blind Man,* Jesus told the world that you must be *born again,* if you would *see* and *enter* the Kingdom of heaven.

In *the Raising of Lazarus,* Jesus said that, as He died and rose again, so will all who have faith in Christ know the power of the resurrection. Jesus Christ shows us His divine authority and power over life and death.

It is faith in these signs that give these events their dramatic significance. Since most people failed to understand the true meaning, Jesus then resorted to direct claims to verify His deity. This was His second manner of teaching.

1. *Jesus taught with Direct Claims*

Jesus knew that He was the Christ, the Son of God, sent by His Father, into the world to redeem the world and to reconcile repentant sinners to God. As evidence of this claim, Jesus used the term *I AM …* at least 14 times. Before examining His claims, it is important to understand the background of the phrase *I AM …*

In the Old Testament, God identified Himself with many terms, beginning with *I AM.* For example, In Genesis 17:1: *I am God Almighty;* in Genesis 28:13: *I am the Lord, the God of Abraham;* in Exodus 20:1, *I am the Lord your God.* In Isaiah, God expressed His omnipotence as Creator: *This is what the LORD says — Israel's King and Redeemer, the LORD Almighty: I am the first and I am the last; apart from me there is no God. (Isa 44:6) … … I am the LORD, who has made all things, who alone stretched out the heavens, who spread out the earth by myself, (Isa 44:24).* These *I AM* phrases define the Lord God Almighty.

Also, in the Old Testament, God chose Moses as the deliverer to bring the Israelites out of physical slavery in Egypt. An angel of the Lord appeared to Moses in the burning bush and Moses turned aside to see *this great thing.* At that moment, God told Moses that He was sending him to Pharaoh to deliver the Israelites. Moses said that the Israelites would ask for the name of the God who had sent him.

Moses said to God, "Suppose I go to the Israelites and say to them,

'The God of your fathers has sent me to you,' and they ask me, 'What is his name?' Then what shall I tell them?" God said to Moses, "I AM WHO I AM. This is what you are to say to the Israelites: 'I AM has sent me to you.'" ... This is my name forever, the name by which I am to be remembered from generation to generation." (Ex 3:13-15)

Therefore, *I AM* is recognized as the eternal name of God.

God, the great *I AM* of the Old Testament, is fully revealed in Jesus Christ, the great *I AM* of the New Testament.

Like God, the Father, the great *I AM*, Jesus, the Son of God, used the same phrase *I AM* in stating directly His claim to deity. The Jews clearly recognized the significance of what Jesus was saying. Therefore, the Jews accused Him of blasphemy for equating Himself with God.

So now, Jesus Christ made seven direct claims to deity. He taught:

- *I am the bread of life. (John 6:35)*
- *I am the light of the world. (John 8:12)*
- *I am the gate for the sheep. (John 10:7)*
- *I am the good shepherd. (John 10:11)*
- *I am the resurrection and the life. (John 11:25)*
- *I am the way and the truth and the life. (John 14:6)*
- *I am the true vine. (John 15:1)*

Since these claims were also rejected, then Christ resorted to teaching in parables, because the Jews *hardly hear with their ears, and they have closed their eyes. (Matt 13:15)*

2. *Jesus taught in Parables*

Jesus taught in parables for two reasons: *first*, because the Jews had rejected His indirect claims as evident in His signs as well as His direct claims to deity; *second*, because the Jews had hardened their hearts.

However, Jesus also explained to His disciples why He spoke in parables.

The disciples came to him and asked, "Why do you speak to the people in parables?" He replied, "The knowledge of the secrets of the kingdom of heaven has been given to you, but not to them … This is why I speak to them in parables:" *(Matt 13:10-12)*

Jesus also taught in parables because a parable is the means of drawing believers and non-believers to the Presence and purpose of God in their midst and the critical nature of their situation.

The Scriptures identify 34 parables of Christ, which contain 23 commands, 16 promises, 41 truths, and 24 warnings, making a total of 104 messages that Jesus has revealed to God's people.

We now move to Christ: our Preacher.

Fifth, Jesus Christ: our Preacher

Jesus was an itinerant preacher, and His entire earthly ministry was dedicated to preaching the good news of salvation through faith alone in Him alone. He preached that no one came to the Father except through Him. He preached that the Kingdom of God had now come, because He, the King of the Kingdom, had come. He preached the necessity of repentance; He preached the power of the Spirit; He preached the need for baptism; He preached about God as our Father and that we should pray with Him and seek to do His will. He preached that we should follow His example and love as He loved.

However, I want to emphasize the message that He preached from the Book of Isaiah.

He [Jesus] went to Nazareth, where he had been brought up, and on the Sabbath day he went into the synagogue, as was his custom. And he stood up to read. The scroll of the prophet Isaiah was handed to him. Unrolling it, he found the place where it is written:

The Spirit of the Lord is on me, because he has anointed me to preach good news to the poor.

He has sent me to proclaim freedom for the prisoners and recovery of sight for the blind, to release the oppressed, to proclaim the year of the Lord's favor.

Then he rolled up the scroll, gave it back to the attendant and sat down. The eyes of everyone in the synagogue were fastened on him, and he began by saying to them, "Today this scripture is fulfilled in your hearing." (Luke 4:16-21)

In this passage, Jesus *preached* three messages.

First, the Spirit of the Lord, who is the Spirit of Truth, is on Me, Jesus Christ. The Spirit leads to truth and the understanding and application of truth. Therefore, what comes from the mouth of such a speaker is the truth from God.

Second, the Spirit has anointed Me (Christ) to preach good news to the poor. The Lord first directed the prophet Isaiah to proclaim this message to the nation of Israel; however, now, Jesus Christ told the members of the synagogue that He was the One who had come to preach the gospel, the good news, to the world. However, the gospel had always been intended as a message for all nations (Gal 3:6-9). The purpose of the anointing by the Spirit is so that the *poor* will hear the good news, gospel, preached to them. In the Scriptures, the *poor* are those in need and requiring aid and assistance. But also Jesus speaks of the *poor in spirit: blessed are the poor in spirit, for theirs is the kingdom of heaven. (Matt 5:3)* The poor in spirit are those who seek the leading of the Spirit of God to empower them. The poor are those who know their needs and turn to God to fulfill those needs.

Third, the Spirit has sent me (Christ) to proclaim this message: freedom for the prisoners, recovery of sight for the blind, the release of the oppressed, and to proclaim the year of the Lord's favor (grace). Again, the *me* initially referred to the prophet Isaiah, but now Christ claimed that the message proclaimed by Isaiah to the nation of Israel will now be proclaimed by Christ to the world.

The message from Christ is that those *in Christ* will be freed of their sins, that those who have been *blind* to the ways of God will be given new *eyesight* through the cross, that those who have been oppressed by the law will find the grace of God available to them,

It is a message about *freedom* in Christ, about *eyes* to perceive God's ways leading to God's Kingdom, about release from the oppression of the law to an understanding of the grace of God, and to know the fullness of God's *grace* and His perfect *favor*.

Christ had come to do everything that was proclaimed by Isaiah: that is why Christ made this statement: *Today this scripture is fulfilled in your hearing.*

But more importantly, Christ is telling the world that He has come, not to the nation of Israel, but to the world.

Because of Love, He came …

    With this understanding of Jesus Christ, we now turn to the Cross of Christ.

Because of Love, He came …

Chapter 4. The Cross of Christ

This man [Jesus Christ] was handed over to you by God's set purpose and foreknowledge; and you, with the help of wicked men, put him to death by nailing him to the cross. But God raised him from the dead, freeing him from the agony of death, because it was impossible for death to keep its hold on him. (Acts 2:23-25)

For Christ did not send me [Paul] to baptize, but to preach the gospel — not with words of human wisdom, lest the cross of Christ be emptied of its power. For the message of the cross is foolishness to those who are perishing, but to us who are being saved it is the power of God. (1 Cor 1:17-18)

I [Paul] have been crucified with Christ and I no longer live, but Christ lives in me. The life I live in the body, I live by faith in the Son of God, who loved me and gave himself for me. (Gal 2:20)

He forgave us all our sins, having canceled the written code, with its regulations, that was against us and that stood opposed to us; he took it away, nailing it to the cross. And having disarmed the powers and authorities, he made a public spectacle of them, triumphing over them by the cross. (Col 2:13-15)

We now address one of the monumental subjects of the Scriptures: *The Cross of Christ.*

However, first, consider the passages at the beginning of this chapter.

The first passage, Acts 2:23-25, presents the truth that the cross was no accident nor the plan of men: the cross was according to *God's set purpose and foreknowledge.*

In I Corinthians 1:17-18, the cross defines the power of God. In another sense, the cross also defines the love of God.

In Galatians 2:20, the apostle Paul stated that Christ lived in him because Paul had been crucified with Christ.

In Colossians 2:13-15, our sins were *nailed* to the cross: therefore, we have victory over sin through the cross.

The Cross of Christ is the defining reason for which God sent His Son into the world. Christ set His face directly to the cross, to die for the sins of the world, to take on our sins, and to make us the righteousness of God.

The Cross of Christ identifies the basis for the forgiveness of sin, for redemption, for reconciliation, for the gift of the Spirit, for salvation, for the resurrection, and for eternal life.

However, as much as we may try, we will never fully understand the significance of the Cross of Christ. To understand the cross requires that we understand the Mind of God and the Love of God, because God's Mind and God's Love are the foundation for God's Cross.

To understand the cross, we would have to have been there for the trials before Caiaphas and Pilate, for the scourging, for the crowd demanding His crucifixion, for the agonizing sight of Christ carrying His cross, for the hammer slamming the nails into His flesh, for the passion and agony of the Son of God, for the cries of Christ to the Father, for the two prisoners on either side, for those who ridiculed Him, for those who mocked and cast contempt on Him, and for the presence of His mother and the apostle John.

Everyone can imagine the physical agony, but no one can imagine the spiritual agony of the separation of the Son from the Father. That divine separation was the ultimate agony.

This much is certain: the Cross of Christ is the heart of the Bible. Christ on the cross, dying for the sins of the world, is the ultimate moment in divine and secular history. For that reason, we must make every effort to understand the Cross of Christ.

To begin with, we can never separate Christ from His cross.

During His earthly ministry, He set His face steadfastly for

Jerusalem, knowing the will of His Father and what lay ahead of Him. The cross was no surprise. Early in His earthly ministry, Christ made this prediction.

Just as Moses lifted up the snake in the desert, so the Son of Man must be lifted up, that everyone who believes in him may have eternal life. (John 3:14-15)

Christ, on the cross, is the supreme example of the love of God.

To understand the cross is the understand love; to understand the cross is to understand light.

For Christ on the cross is the light who came into the world to reveal the truth about God and to glorify His Father.

The passage, John 3:14-15, reveals one of His reasons for His Incarnation, but it also identifies the manner of His death and the purpose of His death. His manner: to be lifted up (crucified): His purpose: so that all who believed in Him would have eternal life. This fulfilled that event foreshadowed by Moses in the wilderness.

For the world enslaved by sin, Jesus Christ is the *Deliverer* and the *Savior* of the world.

The cross was God's instrument to rescue us from this present evil age (Gal 1:4). This cross, this most hated symbol of punishment and suffering, was the fate of the Suffering Servant, Christ our Savior and our Lord.

However, the Cross of Christ was foreshadowed in the Old Testament by at least four events: *first,* the Flood; *second,* the Exodus; *third,* the new covenant; and *fourth,* the sin sacrifice ordained by God.

First, The Flood and the Cross:

The Flood represented God's judgment on man's wickedness and His initial response to sin.

The LORD saw how great man's wickedness on the earth had become, and that every inclination of the thoughts of his heart was only evil all the time. The LORD was grieved that he had made man on the earth, and his heart was filled with pain. So the LORD said, "I will wipe mankind, whom I have created, from the face of the earth — men and animals, and creatures that move along the ground, and birds of the air — for I am grieved that I have made them." (Gen 6:5-8)

Here is recorded wickedness and evil: here is recorded that *The LORD was grieved that he had made man on the earth, and his heart was filled with pain.* Can anyone imagine the Creator of the Universe being grieved and His heart filled with pain! So God determined *to bring floodwaters on the earth to destroy all life under the heavens.*

God's answer to sin was the destruction of that which was the manifestation of sin. However, God resolved never again to destroy all life.

So, for the repentant sinner, God determined to resolve the issue of the sin by a new covenant, whose primary provision would be for the forgiveness of sin. For such a divine ratification, the only suitable sacrificial Lamb would be God's only-begotten Son.

On the cross, a divine exchange took place. On the cross, the righteousness of the Son of God was exchanged for the sins of mankind. We became righteous; Christ became sin.

The Flood and the Cross are remarkably interconnected.

We now move to the Exodus which also foreshadowed the cross.

Second, The Exodus and the Cross:

In the Exodus, God responded to the cries of His people in *physical* slavery to an evil Pharaoh. God chose a *human deliverer,* Moses, through whom God demonstrated His love, His protection, and His provision. God not only set them free from Egypt, but He made provision for a better home and a better future. God ordained a physical kingdom under His love, His rule, and His authority.

The Exodus, a physical event, demonstrated the love and the power of God. God was their Savior: Moses was their deliverer.

Now, consider the Cross of Christ. God's people were in *spiritual* slavery to sin: now, God sent another *Deliverer,* His Son, Jesus Christ, to free His people and to lead them to the Promised Land, which is eternal life in the Kingdom of God.

Therefore, the cross is both a physical and a spiritual event, with Christ as our *Deliverer.*

Next, let us turn to the new covenant for the forgiveness of sins.

Third, The New Covenant (Jer 31:31-34)

The third event that foreshadowed the cross was the new covenant, prophesized through Jeremiah, with five promises: *first, I [God] will put my law within them, and I will write it upon their hearts; second, I will be their God, and they shall be my people; third, they shall all know me; fourth, I will forgive their iniquity; fifth, I will remember their sin no more.*

Six centuries after Jeremiah proclaimed this new covenant, Christ met with His disciples in an upper room in Jerusalem to celebrate the Passover meal in recognition of God's protection, His provision, and the deliverance of the Israelites from Egypt. It commemorated the sacrificial death of the Passover lamb, which was the blood shed for their deliverance from physical slavery.

Now, approximately 1,500 years after the Exodus, the blood of that Passover lamb was to be the blood of Jesus Christ, the Lamb of God, who was both the physical and spiritual Paschal Lamb. Christ, the true Paschal Lamb, was born to deliver and redeem repentant sinners from the sins of the world.

However, this covenant must be ratified through the blood sacrifice, accomplished on the cross *(Heb 9:22).*

Closely associated with the Passover meal was the Feast of Unleavened Bread. The Passover related to blood sacrifice: the companion feast relates to unleavened bread. The Passover required the sacrifice of a lamb with its blood smeared on their doorposts so that the angel of death, sent by God, would *pass over* their houses when He destroyed the firstborn in Egypt. The Exodus contains both the Passover feast and the Feast of Unleavened Bread: the Passover signified *protection*; the Feast of Unleavened Bread signified *provision*.

Christ is the true Passover Lamb; Christ is the Bread of life.

The Exodus takes on a whole new meaning when the Cross of Christ comes on the scene.

By His cross, the Passover was given a new and far greater significance.

That night, when Jesus Christ met with His disciples in that upper room in Jerusalem, the Passover was dramatically and eternally changed. To understand the significance of that change, consider Christ's words that evening.

While they were eating, Jesus took bread, gave thanks and broke it, and gave it to his disciples, saying, "Take and eat; this is my body." Then he took the cup, gave thanks and offered it to them, saying, "Drink from it, all of you. This is my blood of the [new] covenant, which is poured out for many for the forgiveness of sins. I tell you, I will not drink of this fruit of the vine from now on until that day when I drink it anew with you in my Father's kingdom." (Matt 26:26-29)

Christ said that the bread was my body; Christ said that the wine was my blood of the new covenant which is poured out for many for the forgiveness of sin.

The blood of Christ, shed on the cross, ratified the new covenant which God proclaimed through Jeremiah six centuries earlier.

The Passover provided *divine protection*; the Feast of Unleavened Bread ensured *divine provision*.

Christ, on the cross, provided both.

Fourth, The Sin Offering

The sin offering is the fourth event which foreshadows the cross. In essence, a sin offering has three central ideas: *consecration, expiation* (covering of sin), and *propitiation* (satisfaction of divine anger).

Both the Old and the New Testaments confirm that sacrifices represented a symbolic act. Man was obligated because of his sin to present offerings by which he gave another life in place of his own.

Ultimately, such sacrifices lead to the one final and perfect sacrifice of Jesus Christ (Heb 10:11-18).

According to God's command, the animal sacrificed had to be physically perfect; and, through the perfection of this animal, perfection was presented to God. Ultimately, this symbolized the necessity for man to present himself perfect before God by presenting the perfect one in his place (1 Peter 1:18-19). The true Lamb of God, perfect in all regards and innocent of all sin, died for our sins. (John 1:29)

After the animal was selected and presented at the altar, the first act was the laying on of hands by the person presenting the offering. By this act, the worshiper symbolically transferred his sin to the sacrificial animal. The sacrifice symbolically pointed to Jesus Christ who would do for the believer what he could not do for himself. He would take upon Himself sin and guilt and accomplish redemption for His people. (Isa 53:4-12; Matt 1:21)

Christ became the sin offering for us.

However, we cannot complete this discussion of the Cross of Christ without addressing two companion subjects: first, *The Cup of God's Wrath* that Christ prayed would be taken from Him; second, *The Agony of the Cross.*

The Cup of God's Wrath

To appreciate the meaning of God's wrath, we must go back to that evening of the Passover meal and Christ then going to the Garden of Gethsemane to pray to the Father (Mark 14:16-41). Here we will find the meaning of this *cup.*

Here, Christ prayed for two things: first, *if possible the hour might pass from him;* second, *take this cup from me.* However, Christ closed His prayer with these words: *Yet not what I will, but what you will.*

Understand the setting for this drama.

The disciples left, went into the city and found things just as Jesus had told them. So they prepared the Passover. ...

After completing the Passover meal: *when they had sung a hymn, they went out to the Mount of Olives.*

"You will all fall away," Jesus told them, "for it is written: "'I will strike the shepherd, and the sheep will be scattered.' But after I have risen, I will go ahead of you into Galilee."

Peter declared, "Even if all fall away, I will not." "I tell you the truth," Jesus answered, *"today — yes, tonight — before the rooster crows twice you yourself will disown me three times."*

But Peter insisted emphatically, "Even if I have to die with you, I will never disown you." And all the others said the same.

They went to a place called Gethsemane, and Jesus said to his disciples, "Sit here while I pray." Going a little farther, he fell to the ground and prayed that if possible the hour might pass from him.

"Abba, Father," he said, "everything is possible for you. Take this cup from me. Yet not what I will, but what you will."

What is this *cup* that Christ asks to be taken from Him and that He would not have to *drink?*

Here we must turn to two passages from Isaiah 51.

Awake, awake! Rise up, O Jerusalem, you who have drunk from the hand of the LORD the cup of his wrath, you who have drained to its dregs the goblet that makes men stagger. (Isa 51:17)

This is what your Sovereign LORD says, your God, who defends his people: "See, I have taken out of your hand the cup that made you stagger; from that cup, the goblet of my wrath," (Isa 51:22)

This concept of the cup of God's wrath is also discussed in Jeremiah 25:15, Ezekiel 23:33, Habakkuk 2:16, and elsewhere in both the Old and New Testaments.

So what is this cup which Jesus Christ seeks not to drink?

It is God's wrath against the sins of the world, against man's disobedience and rebellion, against all that is evil in the hearts of men.

God's wrath is the perfect manifestation of His holy anger and judgment against sin. In one way, God's wrath is an expression of His holy love. God's expression of divine wrath is the same judgment which we also should have regarding sin.

The Bible declares that all people are *by nature objects of wrath (Eph 2:3)* and that *The wrath of God is being revealed from heaven against all the godlessness and wickedness of men who suppress the truth by their wickedness,* (Rom 1:18). Since Christians have been *justified by His blood, we shall be saved from wrath through Him [Christ] (Rom 5:9).* God's love and God's wrath are fully manifested on the cross, where God's only begotten Son experienced God's wrath on our behalf. On the cross, Christ *drank* the cup of God's wrath against sin. On the cross, God's love for sinners was revealed; in the same way, God's wrath against sin was equally revealed by the darkness which covered the earth when the Son of God died physically for our sins.

The day of the Lord's wrath (Zeph 1:18) is identical with *the great day of the Lord (Zeph 1:14).* In the Last Day, the ungodly will experience *the wrath of the Lamb (Rev 6:16),* Jesus Christ, that will fall on the ungodly at His Second Coming (1 Thess 1:10; 5:9; 2 Thess 1:7-10).

They tell how you turned to God from idols to serve the living and true

God, and to wait for his Son from heaven, whom he raised from the dead — Jesus, who rescues us from the coming wrath. (1 Thess 1:9-10)

So Christ asked the Father: *Take this cup from me.* Yet the Son said to the Father: I have come to do your will. Christ said: *not my will but thine be done.*

The Agony of the Cross

Any discussion of the Cross of Christ requires that we consider the agony of that cross. It is an agony we can only partially understand.

Remember that the Father and the Son are One (John 17:11); on the cross, which was the plan of God, the Father and the Son experienced divine separation. It was that separation that brought tremendous agony to the Son of God.

Why? Because the unity of the Father and the Son, which existed before time began was about to be momentarily broken. That momentary separation brought untold spiritual agony for the Son of God.

The agony was not the shouts of the crowd: *Crucify him.* It was not the rejection of His own people. It was not the desertion of His disciples. It was not the beating by the Roman soldiers; it was not the crown of thorns jammed into His skull; it was not the nails driven into His wrists and ankles. No, it was not the physical and emotional pain.

The agony that He suffered on the cross was the spiritual pain of separation from His Father: that was the agony on the cross.

That separation from the Father led to the darkness for the world and for the Son of God.

Christ, who knew no sin, became sin. Therefore God's wrath will be upon Him. God's wrath led to separation from the Father. That is the ultimate agony of the cross.

So we conclude: the Cross of Christ is the witness to the world of the sovereignty and love of God.

It is fitting that I close with a quote from my friend, Dr. John Stott, regarding Christ and His Cross.

He knew Himself to be Lord of all, but He became the servant of all.
He came to judge the world, but He washed His disciples' feet.

He renounced the joys of heaven for the sorrows of earth.

He was born of a lowly Hebrew mother in a dirty stable in the insignificant village of Bethlehem.

He became a refugee baby in Egypt; reared in the obscure village of Nazareth; toiled at a carpenter's bench; became an itinerant preacher, with few possessions, small comfort, and no home.

He made friends with simple fisherman, publicans; He touched lepers and allowed harlots to touch Him.

He gave Himself away to a ministry of healing, helping, teaching, and preaching.

He was misunderstood, misinterpreted, and became the victim of men's prejudices.

He was despised and rejected by His own people and deserted, in His hour of need, by His own friends.

He gave His back to be flogged, His face to be spat upon, His head to be crowned with thorns, His hands and His feet to be nailed to a common Roman cross---

And as the cruel spikes were driven home, He kept praying—"Father, forgive them, for they know not what they do."

This utter disregard of self in the service of God and man is called love.

This is love which is in deed and in truth.

This is love which leads to life and self-sacrifice.

There is no love without self-sacrifice; there is no church without evangelism.

His character is totally consistent with His claim.

He is truly the Son of God; He is truly the Savior of the world; He is truly King of kings and Lord of lords.

Completing the background doctrines, we now move to an Overview and a detailed discussion of the 30 reasons for the Incarnation.

Part II. The Birth of Christ: The Reasons for His Incarnation

.

Chapter 5. Overview

The 30 reasons for the Incarnation are presented under four headings:

1. *To Serve God*
2. *To Bring Salvation*
3. *To Fulfill The Scriptures*
4. *To Transform The World*

There is no priority for the list of reasons for the Incarnation because to do so would claim to know the mind of God: that is impossible. His ways are higher than our ways; His thoughts are higher than our thoughts. Therefore, the reasons are given without attempting to determine relative importance: all reasons are important.

We begin with the eight (8) reasons for the Incarnation which are related to the purpose: *To Serve God*.

1. To Serve God (8)

Chapter 6. I have come in my Father's name (John 5:43 RSV)

Chapter 7. I have come down from heaven ... to do the will of him who sent me (John 6:38 RSV)

Chapter 8. I must preach the good news of the kingdom of God ... because that is why I was sent (Luke 4:43-44)

Chapter 9. that you may be sons of your Father in heaven (Matt 5:45)

Chapter 10. Anyone who has seen me has seen the Father (John 14:9)

Chapter 11. he will give you another Counselor to be with you forever—the Spirit of truth.(John 14:16-17 RSV)

Chapter 12. I have brought you glory on earth by completing the work you gave me to do (John 17:4-5)

Chapter13. Yet to all who received him, to those who believed in his name, he gave the right to become children of God (John 1:12 RSV)

Because of Love, He came …

Chapter 6. I [Christ] have come in my Father's name (John 5:43 RSV)

For I will proclaim the name of the LORD. Ascribe greatness to our God! The Rock, his work is perfect; for all his ways are justice. A God of faithfulness and without iniquity, just and right is he. (Deut 32:3-4 RSV)

For I [Christ] tell you, you will not see me again, until you say, 'Blessed is he who comes in the name of the Lord.' (Matt 23:39 RSV)

Blessed is the King who comes in the name of the Lord! Peace in heaven and glory in the highest. (Luke (19:38 RSV)

I [Christ] have come in my Father's name, *and you do not receive me. (John 5:43 RSV)*

Jesus Christ said: I have come in my Father's name; then He added this startling qualification: *you [the Jews] do not receive me.* Jesus Christ said: my own people, who should have known about the Messiah and who should have welcomed me—they did not receive me.

The first truth we must understand is this: if we accept the name of the Lord, then we must also accept Christ, the Son of God. As the Son is the image of the Father, to accept the Father is to accept the Son.

We must accept the Son in the same way we *accept* the Father.

But what does *accept* mean? It means many things: to show approval and favor. However, above all, to accept means to express and have *belief* in that person.

We accept what we approve; we accept what we favor; we accept what we believe and what we trust.

Jesus said to the Jews: you don't approve of me; you don't believe in me, and you don't trust me. If you trusted God, the Father, you would have trusted me. Your lack of trust in me shows that you do not trust God.

Second, what is the significance of the name of the Lord? In the Scriptures, the name of God represents all that He is, all that He has done, and all that He is capable of doing. The name of God defines the Person and character of God.

As a result, the Old Testament has at least 16 names for God, each one presenting a unique characteristic of God. Consider them: Elohim (God's Power and Might); Adonai (the Lord God); Jehovah (God's divine Salvation); Jehovah Maccaddeshem (The Lord, thy Sanctifier); Jehovah Rohi (The Lord, thy Shepherd); Jehovah Shemmah (The Lord Ever Present); Jehovah Rapha (The Lord, thy Healer); Jehovah Tsidkenu (The Lord our Righteousness); Jehovah Jireh (The Lord our Provider); Jehovah Nissi (The Lord our Banner); Jehovah Shalom (The Lord, our Peace); Jehovah Sabbaoth (The Lord of Hosts); El-Elyon (The Lord most High); El-Roi (The Lord all Seeing); El-Shaddai (The Lord Almighty); El-Olam (The everlasting God).

However, God has given Himself one specific name which He revealed to Moses, *I AM WHO I AM.*

Then Moses said to God, "If I come to the people of Israel and say to them, 'The God of your fathers has sent me to you,' and they ask me, 'What is his name?' what shall I say to them?" God said to Moses, "I AM WHO I AM." And he said, "Say this to the people of Israel, 'I AM has sent me to you.'" God also said to Moses, "Say this to the people of Israel, 'The LORD, the God of your fathers, the God of Abraham, the God of Isaac, and the God of Jacob, has sent me to you': this is my name for ever, and thus I am to be remembered throughout all generations. (Ex 3:13-16 RSV)

God is the great *I AM*; as God's Son, Christ is equally the great *I AM.* This is the *ego eimi* statement of the Scriptures. When Jesus used that phrase in reference to Himself, the Jews could not have misunderstood Christ's claim to be God Almighty. God in the flesh was among them.

Seven times in the Gospel according to John, Christ described Himself, using that *I AM* formula: *I am the bread of life. (John 6:35 RSV); I am the light of the world. (John 8:12 RSV); I am the gate for the sheep. (John*

10:7 RSV); I am the good shepherd. (John 10:11 RSV); I am the resurrection and the life. (John 11:25 RSV); I am the way and the truth and the life. (John 14:6 RSV); I am the true vine. (John 15:1 RSV)

Now, to these Old Testament names for God, Jesus came to bring a new name, *Father*, which defines a totally new relationship between God and His people. Identifying God as *Father* means that the people of God who have accepted Jesus Christ as Savior and Lord, are now the *children of God.*

Since Jesus Christ had come in the name of the Lord; and, if blessed is He who comes in the Lord, then it would seem natural for the Jews to accept Jesus Christ as the Son of God and as the image of the invisible God.

However, as the apostle John wrote: *The true light that enlightens every man was coming into the world. He was in the world, and the world was made through him, yet the world knew him not. He came to his own home, and his own people received him not. But to all who received him, who believed in his name, he gave power to become children of God; who were born, not of blood nor of the will of the flesh nor of the will of man, but of God. (John 1:9-13 RSV)*

He came to His own, and His own received Him not. *But to all who received Him, who believed in his name, he gave power to become children of God.*

The children of God are those who receive Christ and believe in His name.

Those who reject Christ and deny that He came in the name of the Lord are not the children of God. Such are the created of God, but they are not the children of God.

The acceptance of Christ, the Son, is the acceptance of God, the Father.

The rejection of Christ, the Son, is the rejection of God, the Father.

The Father and the Son are one (John 17:11 RSV).

Consistent with the Old Testament writers, the New Testament also emphasized the importance of names and the close relationship between names and their meaning.

Consider Acts 4:12 RSV: *And there is salvation in no one else, for there is no other name under heaven given among men by which we must be saved.*

In this instance, the name is interchangeable with the reality which it represents. It is clear that salvation is through the name of the Lord.

Blessed is He who comes in the name of the Lord. This One who comes in the name of God is also the One who is the image of the invisible God (Col 1:15). This is the One the Jews rejected.

Christians were described as those who *name the name of the Lord (2 Tim 2:19 RSV).* A true understanding of the exalted Jesus is often connected with a statement about His name. Thus, Jesus *having become as much superior to angels as the name he has obtained is more excellent than theirs. (Heb 1:4 RSV)*

Everyone who calls on the name of the Lord will be saved. (Joel 2:32 RSV)

Therefore God has highly exalted him and bestowed on him the name which is above every name, that at the name of Jesus every knee should bow, in heaven and on earth and under the earth, and every tongue confess that Jesus Christ is Lord, to the glory of God the Father. (Phil 2:9-11 RSV)

Blessed is he who comes in the name of the Lord.
    I [Christ] have come in my Father's name, (John 5:43 RSV)

Because of Love, He came …

Chapter 7. I [Christ] have come down from heaven … to do the will of Him who sent me (John 6:38 RSV)

*All that the Father gives me will come to me; and him who comes to me I will not cast out. For **I have come down from heaven,** not to do my own will**, but the will of him who sent me**; and this is the will of him who sent me, that I should lose nothing of all that he has given me, but raise it up at the last day. For this is the will of my Father, that everyone who sees the Son and believes in him should have eternal life; and I will raise him up at the last day. (John 6:37-40 RSV)*

Consequently, when Christ came into the world, he said, "Sacrifices and offerings thou hast not desired, but a body hast thou prepared for me; in burnt offerings and sin offerings thou hast taken no pleasure. Then I said, 'Lo, I have come to do thy will, O God," (Heb 10:5-7 RSV)

Another principal reason for the Incarnation was that Christ came to do the will of God.

So what is the *will of God* for which Jesus Christ was sent into the world?

The answer is clear: it was to die for the sins of the world; it was to reveal the Father and the will of the Father; it is to seek and to save the lost (Luke 19:10). It is to lose none of all those that God the Father has given the Son and to raise them up on the last day. (John 6:39)

Further, it is the Father's will that all who believe in Christ would have eternal life (John 3:36). As God raised His Son from the grave, so will He resurrect all who have received Him and believed in His name.

When the will of God is considered, two principal aspects of salvation are identified: that we would remain Christ's forever and that we would have eternal life. Nothing can separate us from the love of God which is in Christ Jesus our Lord. (Rom 8:39)

When we become the children of God, we become the resurrected of God; we will be resurrected to share eternal life with the Father.

The Cross of Christ is the basis for redemption and reconciliation: it is also the foundation for the resurrection and eternal life. The truth is that *everyone who looks to the Son and believes in him shall have eternal life.* This understanding of *everyone who looks to the Son* is related to two passages: Numbers 21:4-9 RSV and John 3:14-15 RSV.

The Exodus passage (Numbers 21:4-9 RSV) points to the Cross of Christ (John 3:14-15 RSV).

From Mount Hor they [the Israelites] set out by the way to the Red Sea, to go around the land of Edom; and the people became impatient on the way. And the people spoke against God and against Moses, "Why have you brought us up out of Egypt to die in the wilderness? For there is no food and no water, and we loathe this worthless food." Then the LORD sent fiery serpents among the people, and they bit the people, so that many people of Israel died. And the people came to Moses, and said, "We have sinned, for we have spoken against the LORD and against you; pray to the LORD, that he take away the serpents from us." So Moses prayed for the people. And the LORD said to Moses, "Make a fiery serpent, and set it on a pole; and everyone who is bitten, when he sees it, shall live." So Moses made a bronze serpent, and set it on a pole; and if a serpent bit any man, he would look at the bronze serpent and live.

God punished the sinners, but He made provision for the repentants. In the same way that the people were saved in the wilderness, God made provisions for the salvation of the world through the death of His Son on the cross.

Consider the related passage (John 3:14-15 RSV). *And as Moses lifted up the serpent in the wilderness, so must the Son of man be lifted up, that whoever believes in him may have eternal life.*

The apostle John emphasized that *everyone who believes in him [Christ] may have eternal life.*

The Father loves the Son, and has given all things into his hand. He who believes in the Son has eternal life; he who does not obey the Son shall not see life, but the wrath of God rests upon him. (John 3:35-36 RSV)

The will of Him who sent Me, Jesus Christ, is to die for the sins of the world. It is to make the unrighteous righteous and to make the sinners to become saints. On the cross, there was this eternal divine exchange. On the cross, Christ took on our sins; on the cross, He gave us His righteousness.

Accepting Christ as Savior and Lord makes sinners the righteousness of God.

> *I [Christ] have come down from heaven … to do the will of Him [Father] who sent me. (John 6:38 RSV)*

Because of Love, He came …

Chapter 8. I [Christ] must preach the good news of the kingdom of God … that is why I was sent. (Luke 4:43)

But he said, 'I [Christ] must preach the good news of the kingdom of God to the other towns also, because that is why I was sent.' (Luke 4:43)

We now address another significant reason for the Incarnation: that Christ came to preach the good news of the Kingdom of God which is God's dominion and rule in this age and in the age to come.

We are now living in the power of the Kingdom of God: the Kingdom is present but not fully consummated. It is a reality present now, but it is not always recognized.

The Kingdom of God is one of the most realistic facts regarding this age and this world.

A further truth is that God has established His Kingdom through His Son.

Remember that both John the Baptist and Jesus Christ stated the same message:

In those days John the Baptist came, preaching in the Desert of Judea and saying, "Repent, for the kingdom of heaven is near." (Matt 3:1-3)

Jesus Christ began His earthly ministry by using that same formula.

From that time on Jesus began to preach, "Repent, for the kingdom of heaven is near." (Matt 4:17)

In addition, Jesus taught His disciples to pray that *Thy Kingdom come.* He further instructed them to pray that *your [God's] will be done on earth as it is in heaven.*

Our prayer is that God's will be present on earth as it is in heaven.

This, then, is how you should pray: 'Our Father in heaven, hallowed be your name, your kingdom come, your will be done on earth as it is in heaven. (Matt 6:9-10)

Christ went even further by announcing that the kingdom has come upon you. *If I [Christ] cast out demons by the Spirit of God, surely the kingdom of God has come upon you (Matt 12:28).*

The Kingdom had come because the King had come. The Kingdom is present wherever the King is present. If Christ is within you, the Kingdom is within you.

The kingdom of God does not come with your careful observation, nor will people say, 'Here it is,' or 'There it is,' because the kingdom of God is within you. (Luke 17:20-21)

The Kingdom of God embodies the character of God. As God is eternal and everlasting, the Kingdom is eternal and everlasting.

As God will rule supreme at the end of the Age, so will the Kingdom be supreme at the end of the Age.

The Kingdom is present and will be present in heaven and on earth. This is true because God is the King of the heavens and earth.

We recognize that divine history consists of two ages: this age and the age to come. The Kingdom will exist in both ages.

In this age, the Kingdom of God is the eternal kingdom which shall last until Christ ushers in the age to come. When that occurs, this earth and this heaven will pass away. In their place will come the New Heaven and the New Earth and the New Jerusalem. (Rev 21:1-4)

There are many passages that present a clear perspective of the kingdom of God. *First*, the kingdom of God is an everlasting kingdom (Dan 7:27); *second*, the nearness of the kingdom of God is good news (Mk 7:15); *third*, the kingdom of God is within us (Lk 17:21); *fourth*, we must endure many hardships before we can enter the kingdom of God (Acts 14:22); *fifth*, flesh and blood cannot enter the kingdom of God (I Cor 15:50): *sixth*, only those born of the Spirit will inherit the kingdom of God (John 3:5).

With this perspective in mind, the discussion to the following six areas will expand our understanding of the Kingdom: *1. What is the kingdom of God? 2. What is the purpose of the kingdom of God? 3. Where is the kingdom of God? 4. Who are the citizens of the kingdom? 5. What are the characteristics of the kingdom of God? 6. Why do we pray for the kingdom of God to come to earth?*

1. What is the Kingdom of God?

In the most direct form, the kingdom of God is that spiritual kingdom which God has established in this fallen world, whose citizens are those who willingly accept His sovereign authority and power, and of which His Son Jesus is the glorified Head.

However, the completed kingdom awaits the Second Coming of Christ. When Christ appeared at His first coming, the kingdom was at hand. It was visible in Jesus Christ, who, as the King of the kingdom, was also at hand. His earthly life, crucifixion, and death laid the foundations for His resurrection and ascension to heaven where He is now seated in glory at the right hand of the Father. At His first coming, Jesus Christ came as Suffering Servant and Savior; at His second coming, He will come as King of kings and Lord of lords.

The presence of the kingdom of God in this world forever controls the course of human life and human history (Matthew 13:24-33).

2. What is the purpose of the Kingdom?

The purpose of the kingdom is the *forgiveness, redemption, justification, propitiation, and reconciliation* of all mankind to God and deliverance from the powers of evil. (1 Corinthians 15:23-28)

Therefore, His kingdom is the redemptive rule of God in Christ, defeating Satan and the powers of evil and delivering mankind from corruption. It brings to mankind *righteousness, peace and joy in the Holy Spirit (Romans 14:17)*. By entering the kingdom, the righteous will be delivered from the powers of darkness, *For he has rescued us from the dominion of darkness and brought us into the kingdom of the Son he loves, in whom we have redemption, the forgiveness of sins (Colossians 1:13-14)*.

Forgiveness means that God accepts the death of His Son on the Cross as full and complete payment for the holy and righteous demands of God against sin.

Redemption means that a ransom has been paid for our release from any authority or power other than that of God. That Intervention is through the cross, the atoning sacrifice of Christ, by virtue of which Christ is called our Redeemer.

I know that my Redeemer lives, and that in the end he will stand upon the earth. (Job 19:25)

Our Redeemer — the LORD Almighty is his name — is the Holy One of Israel. (Isa 47:4)

Justification means that God has declared a repentant sinner to be pardoned, declared innocent, righteous and acceptable before Him because of the Cross of Christ.

Propitiation represents two ideas: first, it stands for the atoning death of Jesus on the cross, through which He paid the penalty for the redemption of sinners. Second, Christ has turned aside the wrath of God against sin. Christ is our Advocate, our Redeemer, and He is the perfect sacrifice for the sins of the world.

Reconciliation means that God has taken the initiative in a rebellious and disobedient world that has separated itself from God. Through Christ, repentant sinners are reconciled to God. As such, citizens of the kingdom are to be ambassadors of reconciliation (2 Corinthians 5:20).

These five words, *forgiveness, redemption, justification, propitiation, and reconciliation,* represent the purpose for the kingdom of God.

3. *Where is the Kingdom of God?*

Christ said: if the Spirit of God is within you, then the Kingdom is within you.

Once, having been asked by the Pharisees when the kingdom of God would come, Jesus replied, "The kingdom of God does not come with your careful observation, nor will people say, 'Here it is,' or 'There it is,' because the kingdom of God is within you." (Luke 17:20-21)

Hear the multiple truths: God lives in us; the Spirit of God lives within us; the word of God lives within us; the kingdom of God is within us. We represent the kingdom of God, if the Spirit of God is in us. As we are citizens and heirs of the kingdom, we are to witness to the kingdom. We are the kingdom, living under the authority of our King, our God, our Savior and our Lord, and in the power of the Spirit. We show it by who we are and by what we do. So Jesus said that the answer to the question, *Where is the kingdom? It is within you.*

4. *Who are the citizens of the Kingdom?*

They are the ones who have been justified, redeemed and reconciled to God, who are the saints of the Lord. They are Christ's witnesses and Christ's ambassadors.

They are the ones who do the Father's will.

They are the ones who love and serve God; they are the ones who love their neighbors.

5. *What are the characteristics of the Kingdom of God?*

Scripture identifies at least the following six characteristics of the kingdom of God:
- *It is an everlasting Kingdom.*

Then the sovereignty, power and greatness of the kingdoms under the whole heaven will be handed over to the saints, the people of the Most High. His kingdom will be an everlasting kingdom, and all rulers will worship and obey him. (Dan. 7:27)
- *It is a Kingdom in which all the nations of the earth will be under the Lordship of God.*

They will proclaim my glory among the nations. And they will bring all your brothers, from all the nations, to my holy mountain in Jerusalem as an offering to the LORD. (Isa. 66:19-20)
- *It is a Kingdom which we must seek.*

But seek first his kingdom and his righteousness, and all these things will be given to you as well. (Matt. 6:33)
- *It is a Kingdom that we must enter with childlike simplicity.*

He [Jesus] said to them, "Let the little children come to me, and do not hinder them, for the kingdom of God belongs to such as these. I tell you the truth, anyone who will not receive the kingdom of God like a little child will never enter it. (Mark 10:14-15)

• *It is a Kingdom not of this world.*

When Jesus said that His kingdom was not of this world, He meant that it was not derived from earthly authorities but from God; it is not like a human or earthly kingdom. Jesus said, "My kingdom is not of this world. If it were, my servants would fight to prevent my arrest by the Jews. But now my kingdom is from another place." (John 18:36)

• *It is a Kingdom in which we must be born again to see and enter.*

In reply Jesus declared, "I tell you the truth, no one can see the kingdom of God unless he is born again." (John 3:3-6)

6. *Why do we pray for the Kingdom of God to come to earth?*

The history of civilization does not present a pretty picture. Take every empire and kingdom from the beginning of time. Consider the Assyrians, Babylonians, Egyptians, Romans, and more contemporary times, e.g. the British Empire, and the Third Reich.

The list is endless with few examples of lasting greatness, in which peace among nations or individual human dignity is never realized. Instead, the story is filled with the examples of great empires that have never come close to meeting human interests and needs. The history of empires is a story of abusive power, greed, corruption, exploitation, and cruelty that defies description. Earthly kingdoms, at best, have proven to be bankrupt societies with little regard for any reasonable interest in the life of their citizens. Is that too harsh a condemnation? I think not.

Is it possible that the kingdom which the Scriptures describes is a far better kingdom than man can devise? Is it possible that God's laws and commandments are more beneficial to everyone? Is it possible that God's justice might be more equitable? Is it possible that unity and love might dominate the kingdom? Is it possible that true peace might prevail? Is it possible that man might love his fellow man and that the lion might lie down with the lamb?

The answers to these questions are clear to me.

I pray that the kingdom of God will come on earth because I

believe that His kingdom is the only one which truly offers love and respect among nations and among people.

Therefore, I pray: *Thy kingdom come.*

I must preach the good news of the kingdom of God …
because that is why I was sent. (Luke 4:43)

Because of Love, He came …

Chapter 9. that you may be sons of your Father in heaven (Matt 5:45)

The Fatherhood of God

*You have heard that it was said, 'Love your neighbor and hate your enemy.' But I tell you: Love your enemies and pray for those who persecute you, **that you may be sons of your Father in heaven**. (Matt 5:43-45)*

All things have been committed to me [Christ] by my Father. No one knows the Son except the Father, and no one knows the Father except the Son and those to whom the Son chooses to reveal him. (Matt 11:27)

Yet to all who received him, to those who believed in his name, he gave the right to become children of God— children born not of natural descent, nor of human decision or a husband's will, but born of God. (John 1:12-13)

This reason for the birth of Christ was to introduce God as *Our Father* and to call the redeemed to be the sons of God—the redeemed of the Lord.

In fact, the Fatherhood of God is one of the greatest messages of the New Testament.

God is revealed in a new way which almost defies our understanding. How can the Creator of the Universe have such a personal and enduring relationship with the created?

The Father stands related to the Eternal Son as to none other and finds in the Son the perfect and infinite object of His love. Together the Father and the Son proclaim and send forth the Spirit of God.

But the Counselor, the Holy Spirit, whom the Father will send in my name, will teach you all things and will remind you of everything I have said to you. (John 14:26)

Because of this Trinitarian relationship, the apostles spoke of God as the *Father of our Lord Jesus Christ (1 Peter 1:3; 1 Cor 8:6; Eph 1:17)* as well as *our Father.*

In the same manner, although Christ taught His disciples to address God in prayer as *our Father,* He did not use that form Himself. He spoke of God as *My Father and your Father*; but, at the same time, He distinguished between the relation in which they stood to God and that in which He Himself stood.

It is important to recognize that the early Christian church stated in the initial words of the Apostles' Creed: *I believe in God the Father Almighty.* This is an eternal recognition of the Fatherhood of God.

God the Father is the Father of our Lord Jesus Christ as well as our Father. He is the Father of both His human children as well as His only begotten Son.

In the Old Testament, the term, *God the Father,* is never used. However, it is used 18 times in the New Testament, beginning with John 6:27 and concluding with Jude 1.

In addition, in the Old Testament, the term, *children of God,* is never used. However, it is used 9 times in the New Testament, beginning with John 1:12 and concluding with I John 5:19.

This is a remarkable change in relationship between God and His people in the two Testaments.

In the Old Testament, God is thought of more as the *God of Israel* (2 Sam 7:27; Isa 37:16) rather than of any individual relationship. However, God is referred to as the God of Abraham, Isaac, and Jacob in both the Old and New Testaments (Exo 3:5-6; Acts 3:13).

So this divine relationship in the Old Testament is one in which God is the God of the nation of Israel and has a unique relationship with selected patriarchs, such as Abraham, Isaac, and Jacob. However, we do not find this relationship extending to individuals until the days of the prophets Joel (about 770 BC) and Jeremiah (about 625 BC). In these prophets, we begin to see the evidence of God's individual relationship with the people of Israel and Judah.

In Joel 2:28-32, God announced that He would pour out His Spirit on all people, on all flesh. He also spoke of universal salvation for everyone who calls on the name of the Lord.

Now, in the Jeremiah passage, God proclaimed *that they shall all know me, from the least of them to the greatest (Jer 31:34).*

Behold, the days are coming, says the LORD, when I will make a new covenant with the house of Israel and the house of Judah, not like the covenant which I made with their fathers when I took them by the hand to bring them out of the land of Egypt, my covenant which they broke, though I was their husband, says the LORD. But this is the covenant which I will make with the house of Israel after those days, says the LORD: I will put my law within them, and I will write it upon their hearts; and I will be their God, and they shall be my people. And no longer shall each man teach his neighbor and each his brother, saying, 'Know the LORD,' for they shall all know me, from the least of them to the greatest, says the LORD; for I will forgive their iniquity, and I will remember their sin no more. (Jer 31:31-34 RSV),

So the God of the nation of Israel and of the patriarchs became the God who now has an individual and personal relationship with everyone. That is monumental.

Since God is now our Father, then it follows that we are His children.

That is the great news of the New Testament; that is the great news which Christ came to proclaim.

Yet to all who received him, to those who believed in his name, he gave the right to become children of God— children born not of natural descent, nor of human decision or a husband's will, but born of God. (John 1:12-13)

We, who become the children of God, do so because of the Incarnation. All who receive Christ and believe in His name, to them He gave the right to become children of God, not through any natural descent, but born of God, born of the Spirit.

It is a spiritual birth through our spiritual Father.

He is our Father; we are His children.

Not only so, but we ourselves, who have the firstfruits of the Spirit, groan inwardly as we wait eagerly for our adoption as sons, the redemption of our bodies. (Rom 8:23)

My little children, these things I write to you, so that you may not sin. And if anyone sins, we have an Advocate with the Father, Jesus Christ the righteous. And He Himself is the propitiation for our sins, and not for ours only but also for the whole world. (1 John 2:1-2 NKJV)

And do not call anyone on earth 'father,' for you have one Father, and he is in heaven. (Matt 23:9-10)

Jesus said: I have come to proclaim the Fatherhood of God.

that you may be sons of your Father in heaven (Matt 5:45)

Because of Love, He came …

Chapter 10. Anyone who has seen me [Christ] has seen the Father. (John 14:9)

No one has ever seen God, but God the One and Only, who is at the Father's side, has made him known. (John 1:18)

If you [disciples] really knew me [Christ], you would know my Father as well. From now on, you do know him and have seen him. (John 14:7)

Jesus answered: "Don't you know me, Philip, even after I have been among you such a long time? **Anyone who has seen me has seen the Father.** *(John 14:9)*

This revelation of the Fatherhood of God is a most personal and important reason for the Incarnation.

In addition, Christ now identified Himself directly with the Father: *Anyone who has seen me has seen the Father.*

We have already discussed God as Father. Now, we have the perfect identification of the Son with the Father. Christ is the image of the Father: Christ is the image of the invisible God (Col 1:15).

Christ told His disciples that knowing Him is the same as knowing the Father. From now on, because we have known Christ, we have known the Father and have seen Him. If we have *seen* Christ, we have *seen* the Father. *If you [disciples] really knew me [Christ], you would know my Father as well. From now on, you do know him and have seen him. (John 14:7)*

How did the disciples *see* God? They saw God because they had *seen* the Son of God. To know the Son is to *know* the Father. Here, the word, know, means to become *one with*.

The same truth applies to Christians today. If we *know* Christ, we also *know* the Father. In this context, to *know* Christ is to be in union with Him. Knowing does not mean having knowledge of Christ. In like manner, if we have *seen* Christ, we also have *seen* the Father.

This represents the great truth that the Father and the Son are one. This is the definitive statement that Jesus made which is recorded in John 10:30: *I [Christ] and the Father are one.*

Christ also discloses that the Sovereign God is now the Father of His people: this identifies our relationship with God in a new, personal, and intimate manner.

So the Son came to reveal the Father. Jesus said: if you have seen me, you have seen the Father.

However, at the same time, the Father that we have *seen* is identified as the invisible God. In addition, Christ is the image of the invisible God (Col 1:15). In this passage, God is defined as invisible; this we need to understand.

However, to do so, we must start in the Old Testament, defining the relationship between God and His people.

The theme, *I will be your God and you will be my people,* occurs five times in the Old Testament (Exo 6:7; Jer 7:23, 11:4, 30:32; Eze 36:28). In addition, in the Old Testament, God is recognized as Creator, Sovereign Lord, Judge, Suffering Servant, and King. God does not have a close relationship with everyone. However, in the 7th Century BC, the prophet Jeremiah, in the Southern Kingdom of Judah, received this prophecy from God.

"The time is coming," declares the LORD, "when I will make a new covenant with the house of Israel and with the house of Judah. It will not be like the covenant I made with their forefathers when I took them by the hand to lead them out of Egypt, because they broke my covenant, though I was a husband to them," declares the LORD. "This is the covenant I will make with the house of Israel after that time," declares the LORD."I will put my law in their minds and write it on their hearts. I will be their God, and they will be my people. No longer will a man teach his neighbor, or a man his brother, saying, 'Know the LORD, 'because they will all know me, from the least of them to the greatest," declares the LORD."For I will forgive their wickedness and will remember their sins no more." (Jer 31:31-34)

This new covenant contained five promises: first, *I will put my law in their minds and write it on their hearts; second, I will be their God, and they will be my people; third, No longer will a man teach his neighbor, or a man his brother, saying, 'Know the LORD, 'because they will all know me, from the least of them to the greatest; fourth, I will forgive their wickedness; fifth, I will remember their sins no more.*

They will all know me, from the least to the greatest; to know God is to have a relationship with Him and to be one with Him. *Know* does not mean knowledge about God; *know* means unity with God.

So the Old Testament began with the God of Creation invisible to His people, even though He had an abiding relationship with the nation and with the patriarchs.

However, with the birth of Jesus Christ, we have the fullness of God revealed in His Son. Jesus said: if you have seen me, you have seen the Father. Further, the apostle Paul stated that the Son is the image of the invisible God. Now God is no longer invisible; God is now visible is Jesus Christ.

No one has ever seen God, but God the One and Only, who is at the Father's side, has made him known. (John 1:18)

No one has seen the Father except the one who is from God; only he has seen the Father. (John 6:46)

However, with the crucifixion, death, and ascension of Christ, is God now invisible again?

The apostle John began with the same formula: *no one has seen God ...* but then John goes on to make this startling revelation. *No one has ever seen God; but if we love one another, God lives in us and his love is made complete in us. (1 John 4:12).*

Is God visible or invisible now? The answer is clear: *if we love one another, God lives in us and his love is made complete in us. (1 John 4:12).*

So where is God visible today? He is visible in His people and in His church, if we love one another.

God is no longer invisible; the church is the revelation of God. His children are the revelation of God.

Now, not only is God visible, God is visible as our Father.

Again, the apostle John is the source of this revelation. John stated that those who receive Christ and believe in His name are given the power or the liberty or the freedom to become children of God. If we become His children, it is obvious that God has become our Father.

So, the children of God have dual Fathers, a physical father and a spiritual Father.

Finally, Jesus told His disciples not to call *anyone on earth 'father'*; Christians now have one Father, who is in heaven. He is the only Father we have; He is the only Father we need.

And do not call anyone on earth 'father,' for you have one Father, and he is in heaven. (Matt 23:9)

In the Scriptures, God is called *My Father (47 times), your Father (38 times),* and *our father (24 times).*

The Creator of all, the God of all, who is known as King, Judge, Sovereign Lord in the Old Testament; our God is now going to be known as Father. For that reason, the Son of God came down to earth.

Anyone who has seen me has seen the Father. (John 14:9)

Because of Love, He came …

Chapter 11. he[God]willgiveyouanother Counselor, to be with you forever, even the Spirit of truth, (John 14:16-17 RSV)

And it shall come to pass afterward, that I will pour out my spirit on all flesh … ; And it shall come to pass that all who call upon the name of the LORD shall be delivered; (Joel 2:28-32 RSV)

And when Jesus was baptized, he went up immediately from the water, and behold, the heavens were opened and he saw the Spirit of God descending like a dove, and alighting on him; and lo, a voice from heaven, saying, "This is my beloved Son, with whom I am well pleased." (Matt 3:16-17 RSV)

If you love me, you will keep my commandments. And I will pray the Father, and he will give you another Counselor, to be with you forever, even the Spirit of truth, whom the world cannot receive, because it neither sees him nor knows him; you know him, for he dwells with you, and will be in you. I will not leave you desolate; I will come to you. (John 14:15-18 RSV)

When he comes, he will convince the world concerning sin and righteousness and judgment: concerning sin, because they do not believe in me; concerning righteousness, because I go to the Father, and you will see me no more; concerning judgment, because the ruler of this world is judged. I have yet many things to say to you, but you cannot bear them now. When the Spirit of truth comes, he will guide you into all the truth; for he will not speak on his own authority, but whatever he hears he will speak, and he will declare to you the things that are to come. He will glorify me, for he will take what is mine and declare it to you. (John 16:8-14 RSV)

The giving of the gift of the Holy Spirit is one of the more important reasons for the Incarnation.

God promised this gift in the 8th century BC, through the prophet Joel, who lived in the Southern Kingdom of Judah. It is interesting that God had promised to send His Spirit about one century before the fall of the Northern Kingdom of Israel to the Assyrians in 722 BC and about three centuries before the fall of the Southern Kingdom of Judah to the Babylonians in 586 BC. The circumstances surrounding the promise and the fall of the two kingdoms are unknown, but perhaps God was seeking to equip His people for the trials and tribulations that lay ahead. Whatever the reasons, the two kingdoms did not respond to the promise of the Holy Spirit, until it was too late.

Those two nations ignored the warnings of God. Unfortunately, the same is true today.

People cannot continue to ignore the warnings from God, regarding His will for His people.

Although the nations were unfaithful, God was faithful in His promise to send His Spirit. The gift of the Spirit is one of the great gifts of God. God has given His people many gifts: the forgiveness of sins, the promise of eternal life, life as a child of God. And the list is endless.

With that introduction, consider the four passages at the beginning of this chapter.

The first passage, Joel 2:28-32 RSV, states that God will pour out His Spirit on all flesh before the day of the Lord. The prophecy concludes with this promise: *everyone who calls on the name of the LORD will be delivered (saved).*

The second passage, Matthew 3:16-17 RSV, describes the baptism of Jesus in which the Spirit of God descended on Him. Baptism and the gift of the Spirit are eternally united; the Spirit of God is to be received at baptism.

The third passage, John 14:15-16 RSV, contains several important truths. First, love is expressed in obedience. Second, the Father will send the Spirit at the request of the Son. In addition, Jesus reiterated that message of the callousness of unbelievers: *Be ever hearing, but never understanding; be ever seeing, but never perceiving. (Isa 6:9; Matt 13:14; Mk 4:12; Acts 28:26).* Next, Christ drew a contrast between Christians and the world, by stating that Christians will accept the Spirit, but the world would reject what it does not know. Christ concluded with a reassuring promise: *I will not leave you desolate (e.g. as orphans): I will come to you.* In many ways, this is a divine commitment to the Second Coming of Christ (Rev 22:7, 12).

It might also be a companion to the promise of the angels at the Ascension of Christ: *And while they were gazing into heaven as he went, behold, two men stood by them in white robes, and said, "Men of Galilee, why do you stand looking into heaven? This Jesus, who was taken up from you into heaven, will come in the same way as you saw him go into heaven." (Acts 1:10-11 RSV)*

The fourth passage, John 16:8-15 RSV, defines the three primary roles of the Holy Spirit: first, *he will convict the world of guilt in regard to sin and righteousness and judgment:* second, *he will guide you into all truth;* third, *He will bring glory to me [Christ].*

This is the Spirit of Truth that Jesus promised His disciples; and He has promised us, that, if we love Him and obey His commandments, He would send the Spirit of Truth to be with us forever. This Counselor, this Spirit of Truth, lives with us and lives within us. He is ours forever: that is important to remember.

One of the key questions that must addressed is: *when* do Christians receive the Holy Spirit?

We receive this gift at our baptism which is a public acknowledgment of our receiving Christ as Savior and Lord, our believing in His name, and our commitment to witness to Him throughout our lives.

Baptism is a public acknowledgment of a personal confession of faith already made.

In that regard, baptism is recognized as death and resurrection. We die to the old allegiances and to the old person; we rise up out of the water, a new person, a new creation, and with a new allegiance to Christ. In like manner, we are to baptize all Disciples of Christ so that they also will receive the gift of the Spirit.

Recall that Christ has commanded us: *And Jesus came and said to* them, "All authority in heaven and on earth has been given to me. Go therefore and make disciples of all nations, baptizing them in the name of the Father and of the Son and of the Holy Spirit, teaching them to observe all that I have commanded you; and lo, I am with you always, to the close of the age." (Matt 28:18-20 RSV)

Consider the baptism of Jesus. At His baptism, the Spirit descended like a *dove* on the Lord Jesus Christ. It is obvious that the sinless Son of God did not need to be baptized for the forgiveness of sin. Christ was baptized as an example of what we should do and why we should do it. As the Spirit descended on Him, so shall the Spirit descend on us at our baptism. In fact, the Presence of the Holy Spirit is the confirmation of the validity of our baptism.

At the first Christian Pentecost, Peter challenged everyone to commit their lives to Jesus Christ.

Let all the house of Israel therefore know assuredly that God has made him both Lord and Christ, this Jesus whom you crucified. Now when they heard this they were cut to the heart, and said to Peter and the rest of the apostles, "Brethren, what shall we do?" And Peter said to them, "Repent, and be baptized every one of you in the name of Jesus Christ for the forgiveness of your sins; and you shall receive the gift of the Holy Spirit. For the promise is to you and to your children and to all that are far off, every one whom the Lord our God calls to him." (Acts 2:37-39 RSV)

When Peter finished, he and the other disciples were asked: *Brothers, what shall we do?*

Peter's response was immediate: *Repent and be baptized, every one of you, in the name of Jesus Christ for the forgiveness of your sins.* **And** *you shall receive the gift of the Holy Spirit.*

Notice that forgiveness of sin and the gift of the Spirit are coupled.

Jesus came to bring the gift of the Spirit to all those who call upon the name of the Lord.

he will give you another Counselor to be with you
forever— the Spirit of truth. (John 14:16-17 RSV)

Because of Love, He came …

Chapter 12. I [Christ] have brought you glory on earth by completing the work you gave me to do. (John 17:4)

Father, the time has come. Glorify your Son, that your Son may glorify you. For you granted him authority over all people that he might give eternal life to all those you have given him. Now this is eternal life: that they may know you, the only true God, and Jesus Christ, whom you have sent. **I have brought you glory on earth by completing the work you gave me to do.** *And now, Father, glorify me in your presence with the glory I had with you before the world began. (John 17:1-5)*

This passage emphasizes that the Incarnation of Jesus Christ brought glory to God by Christ completing the work that the Father had given the Son.

That glory of God was revealed in the obedience of the Son to the will of His Father.

In this passage, Jesus said: *I have brought you glory on earth by completing the work you gave me to do.*

What is the glory that the Son brought to the Father? It was in announcing the coming of the Kingdom of God and it was in going to the cross to redeem and reconcile fallen mankind to a relationship with God the Father. To bring glory to God is simply to recognize, worship, and give praise to God because of His splendor and majesty. It is spiritually bowing down before the Creator and Sustainer and Provider and Protector of the Universe. The glory of God is understood by His visible appearance and by His excellence which is unmatched in anyone or anything else. It is the recognition that, with God, all things are possible.

We bring glory to God when we do His will.

What does it mean for us to glorify God? It means simply to give Him the recognition of His love, majesty, power, authority, and sovereignty through worship and praise and by the act of carrying out His will in service to God and to others (1 Pet 4:11; Rev 14:7). We glorify God when we give to Him the worship and reverence which are His (Isa 24:15; 25:3; Ps 22:23; Dan 5:23).

In like manner, we glorify God by our obedience to Christ, our Savior and Lord; we glorify God by our faithfulness as a servant of the Lord; we glorify God as His witness in the world; we bring glory to God when we complete the work He has given us to do.

The faithful and obedient servant is the one who brings glory to God.

We know what God wants us to do; we need to be obedient in fulfilling what He has called us to be and to do.

Christ was glorified by His faithfulness to the cross; Christ glorified His Father in His obedience in doing His will by going to the cross.

In John 12:23, Jesus said: *The hour has come for the Son of Man to be glorified.* Christ was being glorified by fulfilling the work for which the Father had sent the Son to earth. Christ died on the cross, and He was glorified by such an act. Christ was further glorified by being raised from the dead; He was further glorified in His ascension.

We glorify God, not by words, but by deeds.

We will be glorified in loving and serving Christ.

May the God who gives endurance and encouragement give you a spirit of unity among yourselves as you follow Christ Jesus, so that with one heart and mouth you may glorify the God and Father of our Lord Jesus Christ. (Rom 15:5-6)

We glorify God by the degree to which we take up our cross and follow Christ.

We glorify God by the unity within the church.

But what is the work that the Father gave the Son to do?

It was to go to the cross and die for the sins of the world.

It was to exchange His righteousness for the sins of mankind.

Because of Love, He came …

It was to die the cruel death of a criminal, on a cross reserved for enemies.

It was to suffer separation from the Father for a short and unmerciful time.

It was to be sin for Him who knew no sin.

*I have brought you glory on earth by completing
the work you gave me to do. (John 17:4)*

Because of Love, He came …

Chapter 13. Yet to all who received him, to those who believed in his name, he gave the right to become children of God (John 1:12 RSV)

He was in the world, and the world was made through him, yet the world knew him not. He came to his own home, and his own people received him not. But to all who received him, who believed in his name, he gave power to become children of God; who were born, not of blood nor of the will of the flesh nor of the will of man, but of God. (John 1:10-13 RSV)

As previously discussed in chapter 10, one of the important reasons for the Incarnation is that God would be our Father and we would be His children. We now look at this subject from a slightly different perspective than discussed in chapter 10. Since God is our Father, now the Apostle John defines the basis for our relationship with God as His children.

In the Old Testament, the relationship between God and His people is expressed by this phrase: *I will be your God and you will be my people.* That relationship was more with the nation of Israel and with selected Patriarchs than with the individuals.

Now, a new relationship is expressed in the New Testament. God said: *I will be your Father and you will be my children.* This new relationship is that we would be born of God when we receive Jesus as the Christ and when we believe in His name.

It is interesting that this phrase, *children of God*, is used nine times in the New Testament, primarily by the apostle John, but also by the apostle Paul. However, John 11:52 used this phrase, but in a totally different context. In this instance, the passage dealt with the Jewish plot, under Caiaphas, the high priest, to kill Jesus. Therefore, this passage will be omitted in this discussion.

It is also interesting that a similar term, *God's children*, is used three times in the New Testament, making a total of eleven passages which deal with the idea of *children of God* and *God's children*.

An examination of the message in each of these eleven passages will lead to a definition and understanding of this relationship (John 1:12 RSV, John 11:52 RSV; Rom 8:21 RSV; Phil 2:15 RSV; I John 3:1 RSV, 2, 10; I John 5:2, 19 RSV; Luke 20:34-36 RSV; Rom 8:16, 9:8 RSV).

First, John 1:12 RSV, defines the two conditions for becoming a child of God: first, we must *receive* Him, Jesus Christ as Savior and Lord; second, we must *believe* in His name, which means to have faith in Him and trust Him in every circumstance. Under these two conditions, we will be *born of God;* therefore, we will be called the children of God.

Second, John 11:52 RSV expressed God's determination to unite the scattered children of God *and not only for that nation but also for the scattered children of God, to bring them together and make them one. (John 11:52)*

Third, Romans 8:21 RSV states that the creation will also be liberated and be brought into the glorious freedom of the children of God: *that the creation itself will be liberated from its bondage to decay and brought into the glorious freedom of the children of God. (Rom 8:21)*

Fourth, Philippians 2:15 RSV encourages the children of God to be blameless and pure so that they would shine like stars in the universe: *so that you may become blameless and pure, children of God without fault in a crooked and depraved generation, in which you shine like stars in the universe. (Phil 2:15 RSV)*

Fifth, I John 3:1-3 RSV expresses the great love that the Father has for His children.

See what love the Father has given us, that we should be called children of God; and so we are. The reason why the world does not know us is that it did not know him. Beloved, we are God's children now; it does not yet appear what we shall be, but we know that when he appears we shall be like him, for we shall see him as he is. And every one who thus hopes in him purifies himself as he is pure. (1 John 3:1-3 RSV)

The sixth passage, I John 3:10 RSV, defines the children of God by two characteristics: first, the children of God *do what is right*; second, the children of God *have love for one another*.

By this it may be seen who are the children of God, and who are the children of the devil: whoever does not do right is not of God, nor he who does not love his brother. (1 John 3:10 RSV)

The seventh passage, I John 5:1-3 RSV, provides additional insight into the character of the children of God: first, they love God; second, they are obedient to His commands.

Every one who believes that Jesus is the Christ is a child of God, and everyone who loves the parent loves the child. By this we know that we love the children of God, when we love God and obey his commandments. For this is the love of God, that we keep his commandments. (1 John 5:1-3 RSV)

The eighth passage, I John 5:19-20 RSV, describes the understanding that all the children of God have; this understanding is based on God who is *true*. They have a relationship with the One True God who is the Source of eternal life.

We know that we are of God, and the whole world is in the power of the evil one. And we know that the Son of God has come and has given us understanding, to know him who is true; and we are in him who is true, in his Son Jesus Christ. This is the true God and eternal life. (1 John 5:19-20 RSV)

The ninth passage, Luke 20:34-36 RSV, confirms that the children of God will also be the children of the resurrection: they can no longer die, in either a spiritual or physical sense. Again, these promises show the amazing love of God for His children.

And Jesus said to them, "The sons [children] of this age marry and are given in marriage; but those who are accounted worthy to attain to that age and to the resurrection from the dead neither marry nor are given in marriage, for they cannot die anymore, because they are equal to angels and are sons [children] of God, being sons of the resurrection. (Luke 20:34-36 RSV)

The tenth passage, Romans 8:15-17 RSV, states that the children of God have received the Spirit of sonship; therefore, we call God, Abba or Father. The Spirit of sonship makes us heirs of God and co-heirs with

Christ. A further promise is that if we share in His suffering, we will also share in His glory.

For you did not receive the spirit of slavery to fall back into fear, but you have received the spirit of sonship. When we cry, "Abba! Father!" it is the Spirit himself bearing witness with our spirit that we are children of God, and if children, then heirs, heirs of God and fellow heirs with Christ, provided we suffer with him in order that we may also be glorified with him. (Rom 8:15-17 RSV)

The eleventh passage, Romans 9:8 RSV, contains this truth: the children of God are the true offsprings of Abraham which is not by physical descent but by spiritual descent.

This means that it is not the children of the flesh who are the children of God, but the children of the promise are reckoned as descendants. (Rom 9:8 RSV)

From these eleven passages, the following conclusions can be drawn:

To be a child of God, we must receive Christ as Savior and Lord and believe in His name.

It is God's expectation that the creation would be liberated from its bondage to decay and brought into the glorious freedom of the children of God.

The children of God should be blameless and pure, so that they would shine like stars in God's universe.

God's love is so enormous that He should call us His children.

When Christ appears, we shall be like him.

The children of God are known by doing what is right and having love for one another.

The children of God are known by their love for God and their obedience to His commands.

The children of God have the promise of eternal life, which means eternal salvation.

The children of God are the true children of the resurrection.

The children of God are blessed to call God, Father; we are heirs of God and co-heirs with Christ.

The children of God are the true descendants of Abraham.

So this completes the discussion of the Incarnation, as it relates to *God.*

Yet to all who received him, to those who believed in his name, he gave the right to become children of God (John 1:12 RSV).

We now turn to the second series of reasons for the Incarnation: *To Bring Salvation.*

Here the emphasis is on the will of God for the salvation of all who receive Christ as Savior and Lord and who believe on His name.

2. To Bring Salvation (12)

Chapter 14. I have come that they may have life (John 10:10)

Chapter 15. Christ Jesus came into the world to save sinners (1 Tim 1:15)

Chapter 16. I lay down my life for the sheep (John 10:14 RSV)

Chapter 17. Christ died for our sins according to the Scriptures (1 Cor 15:3-4)

Chapter 18. I have not come to call the righteous, but sinners to repentance (Luke 5:32 RSV)

Chapter 19. To preach good news to the poor (Luke 4:18-19)

Chapter 20. For the Son of Man came to seek and to save what was lost (Luke 19:10)

Chapter 21. who gave himself for our sins to deliver us from the present evil age (Gal 1:3 RSV)

Chapter 22. It is for freedom that Christ has set us free (Gal 5:1)

Chapter 23. This, then, is how you should pray (Matt 6:9)

Chapter 24. If you hold to my teaching, you are really my disciples (John 8:31; 13:35)

Chapter 25. If anyone is in Christ, he is a new creation (2 Cor 5:17 RSV)

Because of Love, He came

Chapter 14. I [Christ] have come that they may have life (John 10:10)

Just as Moses lifted up the snake in the desert, so the Son of Man must be lifted up, that everyone who believes in him may have eternal life. (John 3:14-15)

The thief comes only to steal and kill and destroy; **I have come that they may have life**, *and have it to the full. (John 10:10)*

For you granted him authority over all people that he might give eternal life to all those you have given him. Now this is eternal life: that they may know you, the only true God, and Jesus Christ, whom you have sent. (John 17:2-4)

We now come to a statement which represents one of the most important reasons for the Incarnation. Christ has come for our salvation.

I [Christ] have come that they may have life.

There are three aspects of this promise that we must understand.

First, it is only through Jesus Christ that this promise can be fulfilled.

Salvation is found in no one else, for there is no other name under heaven given to men by which we must be saved. (Acts 4:12)

Second, salvation is for those who have received Him and believed in His name (John 1:12).

Third, life is equivalent to salvation and to eternal life.

Therefore, this passage can read: *I have come for their salvation.*

This passage might equally read: *I have come to give them eternal life.*

If there is salvation, there is eternal life. If there is eternal life, then salvation is a reality.

Let us begin by examining the passages at the beginning of this chapter.

The first passage, John 3:14-15, relates to the Exodus when the people murmured against God and Moses, which led to God sending snakes among them. The people, regretting their actions, begged for mercy. So God told Moses to put a bronze snake on a pole and all who looked upon that snake would live (Numbers 21:8-9). This episode foreshadows the cross. Their sin led to consequences which could only be redeemed by God Himself.

Previously, the apostle John had explained that Christ is the living Bread, which is His flesh, which He will give for the life of the world (John 6:51). *I am the living bread that came down from heaven. If anyone eats of this bread, he will live forever. This bread is my flesh, which I will give for the life of the world.*

To say *my flesh* is another way of saying myself. Further, *to eat His flesh and drink His blood* is another way of saying to be united with Him by faith. This powerful metaphor states that eternal life is granted to those who, in faith, come to Christ, accept Him as the Son of God, and enter into an eternal union with Him.

Eating His flesh and drinking His blood are the physical acts which symbolically represent the spiritual acts of receiving Him and believing in Him.

The second passage, John 10:10, compares two types of shepherds or two types of overseers. Although the term, shepherd, is not used in this passage, it is the primary way that Christ saw His earthly ministry. He had come to save; the other shepherd had come to steal and kill and destroy.

The third passage, John 17:2-3, identifies Christ's authority to grant eternal life to those whom the Father had given Him. In addition, the passage defines eternal life as a present reality, when we are united with the Father and the Son. In this passage, to *know* God is to be *one* with Him.

Christ came to give us life; Christ came to save us.

The life that He gives is salvation, which consists of *justification, sanctification, edification,* and *glorification.* We shall look at each of these four terms.

First, Justification:

The truth regarding justification is that which Paul identifies in 2 Corinthians 5:21. *God made him who had no sin to be sin for us, so that in him we might become the righteousness of God. (2 Cor 5:21)* This is one of the more remarkable passages in Scripture. The situation is this: we are sinners; Christ is the righteousness of God. On the cross, Christ took on our sins; on the cross, the righteousness of Christ was *transferred* to us.

Justification means that sins have been confessed and repentance is expressed. As a result, our sins are forgiven, and we are pardoned, declared innocent, and set free. Christ's one act of righteousness brought justification for all people who receive Christ as Savior and Lord.

Justification is God's declaration that the just demands of the Law have been fulfilled in the righteous death of His Son. The basis for this justification is the death of Christ. Paul tells us *that God was reconciling the world to himself in Christ, not counting men's sins against them. (2 Cor 5:19)*

In addition, repentance has the character of death and resurrection; we are dead in sin and made alive in Christ. We die to the old self; we are raised to be a new creation in Jesus Christ.

Repentance involves two decisions and two acts; first, we *turn away* from the wickedness of our former life; second, we *turn to* the new life in Christ. We turn away; we turn to. Both acts must occur for true and complete repentance.

The key is that justification is by faith and not by observing the law. *For we maintain that a man is justified by faith apart from observing the law. (Rom 3:28-29)*

Therefore, faith is considered, not as the work of *man* (Rom 4:5), but as the work and gift of God (John 6:28-29; Phil 1:29).

Not only is Christ's righteousness accounted to the believer, but Christ also dwells in the believer through the Holy Spirit (Rom 8:10), creating works of faith (Eph 2:10). Certainly God's works will be declared righteous (Isa 26:12). If this is true, then the order of events in justification is grace, faith, and works; or, in other words, by grace, through faith, resulting in works (Eph 2:8-10).

Justification is God's work; our response in faith is shown in our works.

We continually remember before our God and Father your work produced by faith, your labor prompted by love, and your endurance inspired by hope in our Lord Jesus Christ. (1 Thess 1:3)

Justification has many positive results: *first*, we are *saved from the wrath of God. Having now been justified … we shall be saved from wrath (Rom 5:9). Second*, we are *saved to: Whom He justified, these He also glorified (Rom 8:30).* Justification is the first step toward final glorification.

Other positive benefits of justification are *peace with God (Rom 5:1),* and *access to God's grace* (Rom 5:2), the redemption of our body (Rom 8:23), and an eternal inheritance (Rom 8:17; 1 Peter 1:4).

Now, justification leads to sanctification, edification, and glorification.

Second, Sanctification:

Sanctification means being set apart, and made holy to love and serve God. It is the process of God's grace by which the believer is separated from sin and committed with undivided devotion to the Lord (I Cor 7:24)

Sanctification is spiritual separation from the world so that we can serve the living God with undivided devotion (I Cor 7:35). Christ was *sanctified and sent into the world (John 10:36).* In the same way, we are to be sanctified and sent into the world. We are in the world but we are to be separated from the things of the world.

Christians are to be in the world, bringing light into the darkness (John 1:3); we are to be in the world but not of the world. We are to be the light of the world, so that those living in darkness will see the light and turn to Christ for forgiveness, pardon, redemption, and reconciliation with God.

Sanctification is accepting the sacrificial death of Christ, and it leads to the purification of believers.

In his epistles, the Apostle Paul noted that God has *chosen* and *reconciled* us to Himself in Christ for the purpose of sanctification (Eph 1:4; 5:25-27; Titus 2:14).

By such acts, we are *dead to sin and alive in Christ* (Rom 6:11).

Sanctification is essentially God's work. We are sanctified by God the Father (Jude), God the Son (Heb 2:11), and God the Holy Spirit (2 Thess 2:13; 1 Peter 1:2). Perfect holiness is God's vision (1 Thess 4:7) and purpose. As Paul prayed: *Now may the God of peace Himself sanctify you completely (1 Thess 5:23)*.

However, in another sense, sanctification is also our work. The Bible states that believers have a responsibility in sanctification. We are commanded to *be holy* (Lev 11:44; 1 Peter 1:15-16); to *be perfect* (Matt 5:48); and to *present your members as slaves of righteousness for holiness* (Rom 6:19).

Writing to the church of the Thessalonians, Paul made a strong plea for purity: *This is the will of God, your sanctification: that you should abstain from sexual immorality; that each of you should know how to possess his own vessel in sanctification and honor, not in passion of lust, like the Gentiles who do not know God. (1 Thess 4:3-5)*

We now address, edification, the third step in salvation.

Third, Edification:

Edification is being led by the Spirit into all truth (John 16:13) and being raised up into maturity in Christ.

Him [Christ] we proclaim, warning every man and teaching every man in all wisdom, that we may present every man mature in Christ. For this I toil, striving with all the energy which he mightily inspires within me. (Col 1:28-29 RSV)

In Galatians, Paul spoke of being crucified with Christ, so that Christ would live in him.

For through the law I died to the law so that I might live for God. I have been crucified with Christ and I no longer live, but Christ lives in me. The life I live in the body, I live by faith in the Son of God, who loved me and gave himself for me. (Gal 2:19-20)

These examples describe how we will be edified: *first,* through faith (Gal 2:15-16); *second,* Christ formed in you (Gal 4:19); *third,* we are to live by the Spirit (Gal 5:16); *fourth,* we will become a new creation (Gal 6:15).

Therefore, if anyone is in Christ, he is a new creation; the old has gone, the new has come! (2 Cor 5:17)

Let us therefore make every effort to do what leads to peace and to mutual edification. (Rom 14:19)

We now move to glorification, the ultimate stage in salvation.

Fourth, Glorification:

Glorification is when we shall have glorified bodies, spending eternity with God. The salvation described here is the result of redemption, reconciliation, the resurrection of the believer, and the gift of eternal life.

The question is: what will our glorified bodies resemble? The Bible states that they will not resemble anything with which we are familiar. Instead, the closest we might come is to understand what the Scripture tells us about the resurrected body of Christ. After His resurrection, His body was physical, but it was not limited by any physical restraints. Somehow, He was recognized. He could be touched; He was visible; He could pass through walls. He was physical without any physical limitations.

And those he [God] predestined, he also called; those he called, he also justified; those he justified, he also glorified. (Rom 8:30)

So, salvation consists of *justification, sanctification, edification, and glorification.*

In every case, grace is the foundation of salvation.

However, we have a distinct role to play, and the apostle Paul defined that role.

For it is by grace you have been saved, through faith — and this not from yourselves, it is the [free] gift of God— not by works, so that no one can boast. For we are God's workmanship, created in Christ Jesus to do good works, which God prepared in advance for us to do. (Eph 2:8-10)

This passage states: God gives us His grace; we respond in faith; the result is salvation.

It is the free gift of God; salvation is not by our works but by our faith.

Paul explained the result of our salvation. It is this: we are God's workmanship, created in Christ Jesus to do good works, which God prepared in advance for us to do. Tomorrow is already planned by God; we just have to show up for work.

When we receive Christ and believe in His name (John 1:12), we receive the power, the liberty, and the freedom to be born of the Spirit which identifies us as a child of God.

We receive justification as a gift; we are sanctified by God; we are edified by the Holy Spirit; we are glorified by God. And the result of salvation is eternal life.

Eternal life

This is the gift of God to all who have received and believed in the Lord, Jesus Christ. It is not eternal existence, which all possess--the saved as well as the unsaved (Dan 12:1-3).

However, eternal life is *Christ in you, the hope of glory (Col 1:27)*. In the Scriptures, hope means certainty. Eternal life is a present reality with its fulfillment in the future.

Eternal life is the result of a spiritual birth (John 3:3; 1:13) and is dependent upon receiving Christ as Savior and Lord. He *who has the Son has the life; he who does not have the Son of God does not have the life (1 John 5:12)*.

Eternal life begins with our acceptance of Jesus Christ as Savior and Lord; it is the result of the new birth from above (John 1:12; 3:3-8). Eternal life has no ending, for it signifies eternal life of the eternal children with our eternal Father.

I [Christ] have come that they may have life (John 10:10)

Because of Love, He came …

Chapter 15. Christ Jesus came into the world to save sinners (1 Tim 1:15)

Here is a trustworthy saying that deserves full acceptance: **Christ Jesus came into the world to save sinners** *— of whom I [Paul] am the worst. But for that very reason I was shown mercy so that in me, the worst of sinners, Christ Jesus might display his unlimited patience as an example for those who would believe on him and receive eternal life. Now to the King eternal, immortal, invisible, the only God, be honor and glory forever and ever. Amen. (1 Tim 1:15-17)*

Here we have a direct reason for the Incarnation: Christ came to save sinners.

In many ways, this is a companion reason to the previous chapter which is a direct statement by Christ. This chapter goes a step further and is based on Paul's understanding of two truths: first, his life as the worst of sinners; second, the unlimited patience of Christ with those who believe on Him and receive eternal life.

This is a most revealing combination of confessions by Paul in which he reveals the depth of his sinful nature and the love of God by which sinners are saved.

The message here is about sinners and sin.

A sinner is a person who is disobedient, stiff-necked, and rebellious to the will and purpose of God. These acts might be either deliberate or unconscious. In either case, the result of sin is spiritual death and separation from God.

Sin is lawlessness (I John 3:4); either the result of personal choice or by the failure to resist temptation.

Sin is to exchange the truth of God for a lie. (Rom 1:25)

The apostle Paul is the classic case of a sinful nature, yet seeking to be faithful to God.

The reason that we sin, even when we seek not to sin, is because sin lives within us as it did within him. (Rom 7:4-20)

Paul knew that life was a matter of facing and winning the spiritual warfare which rages in all of us.

Therefore, we must be strong in the Lord and in His mighty power. We must be prepared to stand firm against our principal enemy, Satan. To do so, we must put on the full armor of God (Eph 6:10-18).

Finally, be strong in the Lord and in his mighty power. Put on the full armor of God so that you can take your stand against the devil's schemes. For our struggle is not against flesh and blood, but against the rulers, against the authorities, against the powers of this dark world and against the spiritual forces of evil in the heavenly realms. Therefore put on the full armor of God, so that when the day of evil comes, you may be able to stand your ground, and after you have done everything, to stand. Stand firm then, with the belt of truth buckled around your waist, with the breastplate of righteousness in place, and with your feet fitted with the readiness that comes from the gospel of peace. In addition to all this, take up the shield of faith, with which you can extinguish all the flaming arrows of the evil one. Take the helmet of salvation and the sword of the Spirit, which is the word of God. And pray in the Spirit on all occasions with all kinds of prayers and requests. With this in mind, be alert and always keep on praying for all the saints.

Notice that the devil's schemes are temptations whose purpose is to separate us from God.

In addition, notice also that our enemies are the powers of this dark world and all the spiritual forces of evil. There is darkness into which the Light of the world has not come.

To overcome the darkness, we have seven pieces of spiritual armor: *the belt of truth; the breastplate of righteousness; the gospel of peace; the shield of faith; the helmet of salvation; the sword of the Spirit.* These six set the stage for the seventh; *to pray in the Spirit.*

Christians: consider your armor: *truth, righteousness, peace, faith, salvation, and the Spirit of God.* The armor is complete only when we pray.

Notice there is nothing on our backs; we face the enemy; we don't turn and run; we stand firm.

Notice also the importance of prayer.

We are not to fall prey to the enemy; we are to resist the temptations of the devil.

However, if we should fall to temptation, all is not lost. Hear the apostle John.

My little children, I [the apostle John] am writing this to you so that you may not sin; but if any one does sin, we have an advocate with the Father, Jesus Christ the righteous; and he is the expiation for our sins, and not for ours only but also for the sins of the whole world. (1 John 2:1-2 RSV)

Consider the evil world into which Christ came (Rom 1:18-31). Paul described the hearts of men then; it is unlikely that they have changed much over the years. We can never ignore the evil; we cannot ignore the wrath of God against godlessness and wickedness.

This passage, Romans 1:18-31, has five principal messages.

The first section, Romans 1:18-20 states two truths: first, that the wrath of God will be revealed from heaven against all *godlessness and wickedness;* second, everyone knows God so that they are without excuse.

The second section, Romans 1:21-23, states two truths: although the world knew God, they did not glorify Him as God nor gave thanks to Him: instead they exchanged the glory of the immortal God for idols and images.

The third section, Romans 1:24-25, states the results of their actions: God gave them over to sexual impurity because they exchanged the truth about God for a lie.

The fourth section, Romans 1:26-27, states the truth that God gave them over to homosexual behavior.

The fifth section, Romans 1:28-32, summarizes the evil condition of depraved minds. They do things that deserve death.

Three times in this passage, Romans1:18-32, *God gave them over (1:24, 26, 28).* God gave them up: it is almost as if God said: if that is how you want to live, then go ahead—I can't stop you. I love you, but I refuse to accept the evil that you practice.

The righteous, holy, and just God will not abide the sins of a rebellious and wicked world.

Yet this is the world into which Christ came to save sinners: that is one purpose of the Incarnation.

Christ Jesus came into the world to save sinners (1 Tim 1:16)

Because of Love, He came …

Chapter 16. I [Christ] lay down my life for the sheep (John 10:14 RSV)

*I [Christ] am the good shepherd; I know my own and my own know me, as the Father knows me and I know the Father; and **I lay down my life for the sheep**. And I have other sheep, that are not of this fold; I must bring them also, and they will heed my voice. So there shall be one flock, one shepherd. For this reason the Father loves me, because I lay down my life, that I may take it again. No one takes it from me, but I lay it down of my own accord. I have power to lay it down, and I have power to take it again; this charge I have received from my Father." (John 10:14-18 RSV)*

This reason for the Incarnation is that based on Jesus Christ as the Good Shepherd who will lay down His life for the *sheep*.

The Good Shepherd is one of the great themes throughout the Scriptures.

We see it in the 23rd Psalm; we see a glorious witness to it in Ezekiel 34:1-31.

Christ, as the Good Shepherd, is the fulfillment of this theme (Eze 34) as He defined the eternal relationship between God and His people.

In addition, Christ defined the ultimate sacrifice of the Shepherd for His sheep: *I lay down my life for the sheep*. No Shepherd ever made that promise; no Shepherd ever fulfilled that promise.

God said: I will be your God and you will be my people. God said: I will be your Shepherd and you will be my sheep (Eze 34). The same relationship is dramatically shown in the role of Shepherd and sheep.

First, consider the role of shepherds in Israel. Judaism devalued the role of shepherds so much that people were forbidden to buy wool, milk, or meat from shepherds. Civic privileges were denied them; worship in the Temple was forbidden. They were outcasts in their own society. The Midrash on the 23rd Psalm had this comment: *There is no position in the world as despised as that of a shepherd.*

And yet that is the title that God choose and that is the title that Christ chooses. Consider how the Scriptures consider shepherds.

We begin with the episode of David, as a shepherd, who became the great king of Israel. We find his expression of his love for God in the 23rd Psalm RSV.

The LORD is my shepherd, I shall not want; he makes me lie down in green pastures. He leads me beside still waters; he restores my soul. He leads me in paths of righteousness for his name's sake. Even though I walk through the valley of the shadow of death, I fear no evil; for thou art with me; thy rod and thy staff, they comfort me. You prepare a table before me in the presence of my enemies; You anoint my head with oil, my cup overflows. Surely goodness and mercy shall follow me all the days of my life; and I shall dwell in the house of the LORD forever.

This Psalm is so familiar that we are likely to miss the truths about God and our relationship with Him.

However, listen to what David said: as long as the Lord is my shepherd, I shall not be in want. Look what my Shepherd provides: green pastures and quiet waters. Not only that, but my Shepherd restores my soul. My Shepherd also leads me in paths of righteousness for his name's sake. Even if I face the most terrible and frightening of situations, I will fear no evil, for my Shepherd is with me. His rod protects me against evil; His staff leads and comforts me. God is with me even in the midst of my enemies. My Shepherd loves me so much that He anoints my head with oil. Because of this, my cup overflows. Surely the goodness and love of my Shepherd will be with me forever. The ultimate promise: I will dwell in the house of the LORD forever.

Second, this theme of shepherd is reinforced by the understanding of God as the Shepherd of His people (Ezekiel 34:1-31). When God saw that the rulers, the shepherds of Israel, were abusing the people, God determined that He would be the Shepherd of the flock, the nation.

For this is what the Sovereign LORD says: I myself will search for my sheep and look after them. (Ezek 34:11 RSV)

In the end of that passage, God said that you are my sheep, and I, your God, will provide for you.

You my sheep, the sheep of my pasture, are people, and I am your God, declares the Sovereign LORD. (Ezek 34:31 RSV)

Third, we recognize that the birth of Christ was announced to shepherds; it was not announced to kings or to the high priest. The wise men from the East *saw* the star; the shepherds *saw* the star. However, Herod and the Jewish leaders did not *see* the star. God revealed Himself to the shepherds: those considered outcasts in their own society.

And in that region there were shepherds out in the field, keeping watch over their flock by night. And an angel of the Lord appeared to them, and the glory of the Lord shone around them, and they were filled with fear. And the angel said to them, "Be not afraid; for behold, I bring you good news of a great joy which will come to all the people; for to you is born this day in the city of David a Savior, who is Christ the Lord." (Luke 2:8-11 RSV)

So, this Old Testament theme of the shepherd is replicated in the New Testament, in which the Son of God declares that He will be the Good Shepherd who will lay down His life for the sheep. It goes far beyond caring for the sheep, protecting them, and providing for them. No, now the Good Shepherd will die for the sheep so that they will have eternal life.

This is the fullness of the Good Shepherd, who is Jesus Christ.

Jesus linked His divine character and divine nature with the most despised occupation in Israel.

Now, considered the character of sheep.

Sheep are curious but extremely dumb animals; there are few animals as dumb as sheep. They will wander into areas of great danger. Sometimes, they will wander down the side of a cliff, from which it is impossible to return. In addition, sheep are defenseless animals; they cannot protect themselves against any other animals. They must rely on the shepherd with his rod and his staff. The rod is to protect; the staff is to lead.

Sheep are generally content to be in the same field with their shepherd; in the same way, Christians are comforted by the very presence of the Lord. As with the shepherd and the sheep, Jesus is our Door; nothing can touch our lives without touching Him also. He spiritually becomes the living door of the sheepfold. He is the door for the sheep, and He puts his body between the defenseless sheep and ravenous animals or thieves.

The shepherd is the provider and the protector; the defenseless sheep must rely upon the shepherd for food and protection. Christ came to protect and provide for His sheep. More importantly, the Good Shepherd came to die for them.

I [Christ] lay down my life for the sheep (John 10:14 RSV)

Because of Love, He came …

Chapter 17. Christ died for our sins according to the Scriptures (I Cor 15:3)

*For what I [Paul] received I passed on to you as of first importance: that **Christ died for our sins according to the Scriptures**, that he was buried, that he was raised on the third day according to the Scriptures, (1 Cor 15:3-4)*

Just as Moses lifted up the snake in the desert, so the Son of Man must be lifted up, that everyone who believes in him may have eternal life. (John 3:14-15)

Now we address one of the most monumental acts in all of human and divine history: the Cross of Christ. This is one of the most important reasons for the Incarnation.

In the previous chapter, we saw the image of Christ as the Good Shepherd who laid down His life for the sheep. Here we have another expression of that same truth; Christ came to die for our sins.

The Cross of Christ is the centerpiece of the Scriptures; it is the moment to which all the Scriptures point and it is the moment from which all the Scriptures follow.

The Cross of Christ is the centerpiece of the gospel of Christ.

Christ was condemned to death in a manner reserved for criminals who were enemies of the Roman Empire and the Jewish rulers. Christ was judged guilty of sedition in the Roman court by claiming to be a king. He was condemned by the Jewish rulers on a charge of blasphemy, by claiming to be one with God. Both the Roman court and the Jewish court directly and indirectly condemned the Son of God to death.

However, God sent His Son into the world to save the world through Him. Christ is the Light that came into world to dispel the darkness and bring those in darkness into His marvelous light.

God sent His Son to die on a criminal's cross; Christ was to suffer for those who shouted *"crucify him; crucify him."*

He was love in the face of hatred. He was God incarnate, rejected and despised.

He was and is the Savior of the world, yet considered a blasphemer and an enemy of God.

He was a King who was willing to die for those who refused to love and serve Him.

He was a Servant, willing to suffer by taking on the iniquities of the world.

He was and is the Righteous One of God, who was willing to exchange His righteousness for our sins.

He is the Source of the resurrection; He is the Agent of eternal life.

How did He die? He died physically on a Roman cross for the sins of the world.

Why did He die? He died to redeem and reconcile sinners with a holy and righteous God.

What are the benefits of His death? He who knew no sin became sin for us. On the cross, the Righteous One of God took on our sins and gave us His righteousness. We became righteous; He became sin. In those totally dark moments, He accepted separation from His Father as an expression of God's love for sinners.

We become the righteousness of God because Christ died for us.

He became sin for us because He died for us, in obedience to the will of His Father.

There is life and there is death.

Now we must understand that there are two kinds of lives through two kinds of births (physical and spiritual); in addition, there are two kinds of death (physical and spiritual).

There is physical birth based on human will and human acts. There is also spiritual birth which is being *born again*, being born of God (John 1:12; 3:3, 5). The spiritual birth leads to two truths: we become a child of God who becomes our spiritual Father.

If we are only born physically, then we will never know the joy of God as Father. We would never be able to call God *our Father.*

Further, there is a physical death and a spiritual death. A physical death, with a spiritual birth, will lead to the resurrection of the body and eternal life with God. However, spiritual death is eternal separation from God.

So, there are two conclusions.

First, if a person is born only physically, then he will die twice, physically and spiritually.

Second, if a person is born twice, spiritually and physically, he will only die once, physically.

We need to be born twice, born again, born from above, born spiritually, born of God (John 1:12-13).

The spiritual birth is based on the truth that *Christ died for our sins according to the Scriptures.*

He died for our sins.

We say this truth so often; however, I question whether the full significance of that statement is truly understood. I am still grappling with the full understanding of it. It should be written on our hearts.

There are two additional truths that follow from this one truth: *Christ died for our sins according to the Scriptures.* First, His death shows the seriousness of sin. My sin is so serious that it required God Himself in the flesh to pay the full price for my redemption. That is an enormous price; there is no greater payment that could be made. Christ died for me; Christ died for you.

Second, His death shows the unbelievable magnitude of God's love. If we want to understand the love of God, look at the cross. There is no greater expression of love: look at the cross.

Finally, we must recognize that the death of Christ was not the plan of man or the will of man. Consider Peter's speech at the first Christian Pentecost.

Men of Israel, listen to this: Jesus of Nazareth was a man accredited by God to you by miracles, wonders and signs, which God did among you through him, as you yourselves know. This man was handed over to you by God's set purpose and foreknowledge; and you, with the help of wicked men, put him to death by nailing him to the cross. But God raised him from the dead, freeing him from the agony of death, because it was impossible for death to keep its hold on him. (Acts 2:22-24)

The Cross of Christ was according to *God's set purpose and foreknowledge.*

God, who sent His only begotten Son to the Cross, *raised him from the dead, freeing him from the agony of death.*

The death of Christ and the resurrection of Christ were both according to the plan of God. The purpose: to redeem and reconcile sinners to a holy God.

Christ died for our sins according to the Scriptures (I Cor 15:3).

Because of Love, He came …

Chapter 18. I have not come to call the righteous, but sinners to repentance. (Luke 5:32 RSV)

And the Pharisees and their scribes murmured against his disciples, saying, "Why do you eat and drink with tax collectors and sinners?" And Jesus answered them, "Those who are well have no need of a physician, but those who are sick; **I have not come to call the righteous, but sinners to repentance."** *(Luke 5:30-32 RSV)*

Teach me what I [Job] do not see; if I have done iniquity, I will do it no more. Will he then make requital to suit you, because you reject it? (Job 34:32-33 RSV)

Therefore I [God] will judge you, O house of Israel, every one according to his ways, says the Lord GOD. Repent and turn from all your transgressions, lest iniquity be your ruin. Cast away from you all the transgressions which you have committed against me, and get yourselves a new heart and a new spirit! Why will you die, O house of Israel? For I have no pleasure in the death of any one, says the Lord GOD; so turn, and live. (Ezek 18:30-32 RSV)

From that time Jesus began to preach, "Repent, for the kingdom of heaven is near." (Matt 4:17 RSV)

Christ now identified another important reason for the Incarnation--the salvation of repentant sinners.

Before addressing that subject, let us consider the passages at the beginning of this chapter.

The first passage, Luke 5:31-32 RSV, raises the question of why Christ and His disciples associated with riff-raff, the rejected of Jewish society. To begin with, the question raised by the Pharisees demonstrates a righteous judgment on others. How does any human being know who is a sinner? However, Jesus answered them by stating that He had come to call sinners to repentance.

The second passage, Job 34:32-33 RSV, is Job's plea to God to tell him what he has done wrong, so that that wrong will not be repeated. Job knows that God will reward those who are willing to repent. God will not acknowledge those who refuse to repent.

The third passage, Ezekiel 18:30-32 RSV, identifies God as Judge, calling on His people to repent and turn away from all their sin. If not, their sins will lead to their downfall. Sinners are to exchange the sin in their lives for a new heart and a new spirit. God calls for His people to repent so that they can be saved.

The fourth passage, Matthew 4:17 RSV, is Christ's call to repentance, because the Kingdom of heaven is near and the King of the kingdom is present in His Person.

Christ presents two themes in this passage (Luke 5:32): sinners and repentance.

Who is a *sinner?* A sinner is someone who has deliberately or unintentionally separated themselves from a holy and righteous God. Therefore, a sinner is a spiritually separated person. He is one who is rebellious, obstinate, disobedient, and stiff-necked. He is one who knows the truth and rejects the truth; he is one who exchanges the truth for a lie (Rom 1:25). He is one who is aligned with Satan, who may even worship Satan: he is a person who refuses to change. He is one who enjoys evil, who loves the darkness, and whose deeds are evil. It is an evil person with no concept of righteousness and without any desire to be righteous. Such a person is lawless.

Since sin is natural to mankind, every person is a sinner (Rom 3:23 RSV): *since all have sinned and fall short of the glory of God.*

Every one who commits sin is guilty of lawlessness; sin is lawlessness. (1 John 3:4 RSV)

One of the major elements of the gospel of Christ is this: *He [Christ] who knew no sin became sin for us. But God shows his love for us in that while we were yet sinners Christ died for us. (Rom 5:8 RSV)*

Next, what is *repentance?* Repentance means to acknowledge sin, to confess sin, to make restitution for sin, and to *turn away* from sin. That is the first step, but that is not all. Repentance must include *turning to* God. It must include both *turning away* and *turning to.*

It is an earnest desire to be redeemed and reconciled to God. It is a quest for restoration.

It is an earnest desire to reestablish the relationship with God that was broken by sin.

It is to acknowledge that Jesus Christ is our Advocate with the Father if we do sin.

My little children, I am writing this to you so that you may not sin; but if any one does sin, we have an advocate with the Father, Jesus Christ the righteous; and he is the expiation for our sins, and not for ours only but also for the sins of the whole world. (1 John 2:1-2 RSV)

The Book of Amos, chapter 4, contains one of the more regrettable passages in the Scriptures. Here God described actions that demanded correction. The Israelites did not repent: four times, God said: *yet you have not returned to me, declares the LORD. (Amos 4:6, 8, 9, 10 RSV)*

When we should return to God, we should return to God.

However, one of the more significant messages regarding repentance is found in the three stories in the parable in Luke 15:1-32 RSV.

The first story is about a shepherd who had 100 sheep and one is lost in the *far country.* The second story is about a woman with ten coins and one is lost at *home.* The third story is about a man who has two sons: one is lost in the *far country* and one is lost at *home.*

The three stories are interrelated; the first two stories set up the third.

This parable is about the *lost* being *found:* about *coming to our senses* which is a form of repentance.

The stories are about rejoicing in heaven when a sinner repents.

The first story is about a shepherd, rejoicing when he finds his *lost sheep.*

The second story is about a woman, rejoicing when she finds her *lost coin.*

The third story is about a Father, who loves His two sons, even when both are *lost.*

It is about one son, *coming to his senses:* It's about another son whose bitterness prevents forgiveness.

It is about one son, *lost in a far country*; it's about another son, *lost at home.*

The first story, about the shepherd and his sheep, ends: *Just so, I tell you, there will be more joy in heaven over one sinner who repents than over ninety-nine righteous persons who need no repentance. (Luke 15:7 RSV)*

The second story, about the woman and her ten coins, ends: *Just so, I tell you, there is joy before the angels of God over one sinner who repents.(Luke 15:10 RSV)*

The third story is about a man who has two sons. The younger son asked for his inheritance which his father gave him. Luke tells us the rest of the story.

The younger son then went to a far country where he *squandered his property in loose living. And when he had spent everything, a great famine arose in that country, and he began to be in want. So he went and joined himself to one of the citizens of that country, who sent him into his fields to feed swine. And he would gladly have fed on the pods that the swine ate; and no one gave him anything. But when he came to himself he said, 'How many of my father's hired servants have bread enough and to spare, but I perish here with hunger! I will arise and go to my father, and I will say to him, "Father, I have sinned against heaven and before you; I am no longer worthy to be called your son; treat me as one of your hired servants."' 20 And he arose and came to his father.*

When he came to himself may well be an appropriate way to define repentance.

But while he was yet at a distance, his father saw him and had compassion, and ran and embraced him and kissed him. And the son said to him, 'Father, I have sinned against heaven and before you; I am no longer worthy to be called your son.'

Consider the reaction of the father to the son; *filled with compassion for him; he ran to his son, embraced him and kissed him.*

The son said to him, 'Father, I have sinned against heaven and before you. I am no longer worthy to be called your son.'

Consider the confession and the repentance of the son.

But the father said to his servants, 'Bring quickly the best robe, and put it on him; and put a ring on his hand, and shoes on his feet; and bring the fatted calf and kill it, and let us eat and make merry; for this my son was dead, and is alive again; he was lost, and is found.' And they began to make merry. (Luke 15:13-24 RSV)

Notice how the father described his son: *dead and is alive again; was lost and is found.* Is that the order in which you would define the return of a lost son? However, it is the correct order in repentance. We are dead in sin and now alive in Christ; we were among the lost, but Christ has found us. Christ came to seek and save the lost.

The story, by every right, should end there, with rejoicing and the father and the son united. However, Jesus continued; there is the older son, *lost at home.*

Notice the anger in the older son: he doesn't call the younger son his brother. No, he said: *this son of yours*—not my brother.

My son, the father said, 'you are always with me, and everything I have is yours.'

This story ends with this statement: *But we had to celebrate and be glad, because this brother of yours was dead and is alive again; he was lost and is found. (Luke 15:32 RSV)*

And so the parable ends.

One son, lost in a far country, repented and came home. The older son, lost at home, did not repent and remained angry at both the father and his brother.

However, heaven rejoices when a sinner comes home; they throw a big party.

> *I [Christ] have not come to call the righteous, but sinners to repentance. (Luke 5:32 RSV)*

Because of Love, He came …

Chapter 19. To preach good news to the poor (Luke 4:18)

*The Spirit of the Lord is on me, because he has anointed me **to preach good news to the poor**. He has sent me to proclaim freedom for the prisoners and recovery of sight for the blind, to release the oppressed, to proclaim the year of the Lord's favor. (Luke 4:18-19)*

Luke 4:16-19 records Christ's presence at the synagogue in Nazareth on the Sabbath, and the scroll of the prophet Isaiah was handed to Him.

The Spirit of the Sovereign LORD is on me, because the LORD has anointed me to preach good news to the poor. He has sent me to bind up the brokenhearted, to proclaim freedom for the captives and release from darkness for the prisoners, to proclaim the year of the LORD's favor and the day of vengeance of our God, to comfort all who mourn, and provide for those who grieve in Zion — to bestow on them a crown of beauty instead of ashes, the oil of gladness instead of mourning, and a garment of praise instead of a spirit of despair. They will be called oaks of righteousness, a planting of the LORD for the display of his splendor. (Isa 61:1-3)

The passage from Luke is a statement from the prophecy in Isaiah 61:1-3. Christ has come in fulfillment of that prophecy.

That passage contains several important subjects, e.g. the good news which Christ is to preach: This is the gospel of Christ, which is the good news regarding the love of God. This good news is to be given to the poor and to the brokenhearted so that captives would be freed and that prisoners in darkness would be released from that darkness and that those who mourn would be comforted. There is to come, the great day of the LORD's favor, but there is also to be the day of vengeance of God. Above all, and this is the good news: there will be beauty instead of ashes (mourning), gladness instead of mourning, praise instead of despair. Those who turn to the Lord will be called oaks of righteousness, the planting of the Lord. All this will occur so that the splendor of God will be displayed.

Before examining this passage further, it is helpful to know something of the prophet Isaiah, whom God anointed with the Holy Spirit and who predicted the coming of the Messiah. Isaiah was born in Jerusalem in a family that was related to the royal house of Judah. He spent his early years as an official, serving King Uzziah, who died in 740 BC. God told Isaiah that his ministry, between 740 and 701 BC, would be one of judgment, which the people would likely reject. It is interesting that Isaiah's ministry preceded the destruction of both the Northern Kingdom of Israel, 722 BC, by the Assyrians and the Southern Kingdom of Judah, 586 BC, by the Babylonians. Isaiah's prophesies of the judgment of God on both kingdoms were ignored; both kingdoms failed to take the word of the Lord seriously. So the consequences were evident; no nation or any individual is exempt from God's punishment for unrepentant sin. The wrath of God is real; to ignore divine warnings is a dangerous thing. Both kingdoms perished: never to rise again.

As with Isaiah, Jesus found in these words the same failure to repent and return to God.

In them is fulfilled the prophecy of Isaiah: 'You will be ever hearing but never understanding; you will be ever seeing but never perceiving. For this people's heart has become calloused; they hardly hear with their ears, and they have closed their eyes. Otherwise they might see with their eyes, hear with their ears, understand with their hearts and turn, and I would heal them.' (Matt 13:14-15)

Although there are many subjects in the Isaiah passage, we will focus on the phrase: *because he has anointed me to preach good news to the poor.*

First, notice the *anointing.* Second, what is the *good news?* Third, who are the *poor?*

First, anointing is to select, authorize, and consecrate an individual for a specific service or ministry. In the Old Testament, the person anointed then *belongs to God*, as *the Lord's anointed, God's anointed, My anointed, Your anointed, or His anointed.* In the New Testament, Christ's disciples are designated as anointed because they were God's own, set apart and commissioned for His service.

Now it is God who makes both us and you stand firm in Christ. He anointed us, set his seal of ownership on us, and put his Spirit in our hearts as a deposit, guaranteeing what is to come. (2 Cor 1:21-22)

Now, we address the *good news*, which is the *gospel of Jesus Christ.*

The gospel of Christ is one of the greatest messages in Scripture, containing the ultimate divine truths for Christians in particular and for the world in general.

The gospel offers the reunion of redeemed man with the holy God.

Genesis 22:15-18 identifies the *universal* character of the gospel: *through your offspring all nations on earth will be blessed. Through your [Abraham's] offspring* means that this blessing will come through Jesus Christ: notice that *offspring* is singular and directly refers to Jesus Christ (Gal 3:16).

The proof that Christ is the Offspring of Abraham is given in the New Testament which begins with these words: *A record of the genealogy of Jesus Christ the son of David, the son of Abraham: (Matt 1:1).* This passage identifies Jesus Christ as the son of Abraham, the *offspring* through whom all the nations will be blessed. Obviously, Jesus Christ is not the divine son of Abraham, but the One who is descended physically from Abraham. Further, God identifies the importance of obedience. The obedience of Abraham is the reason that the gospel was first announced through Abraham (Gal 3:6-9). In addition, the word, *blessed*, is synonymous with *justified,* which means pardoned, declared innocent, and set free. Christ is the basis of our justification that brings redemption and reconciliation with God.

God, acting through Christ, is the Origin of the gospel of Christ. In like manner, Christ is the Source of justification, leading to salvation and eternal life.

As the apostle Paul stated: Christ, on the cross, justified all mankind and thereby brought life (salvation) for all men. *Consequently, just as the result of one trespass was condemnation for all men, so also the result of one act of righteousness was justification that brings life [salvation] for all men. (Rom 5:18)*

Paul, in 2 Corinthians 4:4, refers to the gospel of Christ as *the gospel of the glory of Christ.*

2 Timothy 1:9-10 presents the character of the gospel, the purpose of the gospel, and the result, which are the power of the resurrection and eternal life. *The gospel is the light shining in the darkness of this world, and the light brings salvation (life) and the promise of immortality, which is the power of the resurrection, giving eternal life to everyone who believes.* The gospel is the light of God shining in the darkness; the gospel brings forgiveness, salvation, resurrection, and eternal life to everyone who believes.

These passages attest to the power and importance of the gospel of Christ to all people and all nations throughout history.

In Scripture, the title most commonly used for the gospel is the *gospel of Christ,* which is used 8 times: *Rom 15:19; I Cor 9:12; 2 Cor 2:12; 2 Cor 9:13; 2 Cor 10:14; Gal 1:7; Phil 1:27; I Thess 3:2.* In addition, three other titles are the *gospel of His Son (Rom 1:9), the gospel of the glory of Christ (2 Cor 4:4),* and the *gospel of our Lord Jesus Christ (2 Thess 1:8).*

Further, the Scriptures have seven other titles for the gospel: *The Gospel of the Kingdom (Matt 24:14); The Gospel of God's grace (Acts 20:24); The Gospel of God (Rom 1:1); The Gospel of your salvation (Eph 1:13); The Gospel of Peace (Eph 6:15); The glorious Gospel of the blessed God (1 Tim 1:11); The eternal Gospel (Rev 14:6).* However, the predominant title for the gospel is *the gospel of Christ;* therefore, this title, will be used in this book.

Second, what is the gospel of Christ?

The gospel of Christ is *good news from God which brings great joy to all who hear and receive.* However, the Bible contains both good news and bad news; it has good news for the righteous; it has bad news for unrepentant, rebellious, and disobedient sinners.

In all respects, the *gospel of Christ* is the centerpiece of Scripture.

The *gospel of Christ* includes the truth announced to Abraham, the promise of the Holy Spirit, the new covenant (Jeremiah 31:31-34) for the forgiveness of sins, the Incarnation of Jesus Christ, the spiritual birth, the earthly ministry of Christ, the coming of the Holy Spirit, the

Cross of Christ, the resurrection, the ascension of Christ, the second coming of Christ, the general resurrection, the Final Judgment, and the coming of a New Heaven and a New Earth, and the New Jerusalem.

Third, who are the *poor?*

The poor are those who might be considered to have some deficiency, which could be either physical or spiritual. However, those who are poor in spirit will be rich in the things of God. Poor in ourselves may well lead to the riches of God.

In the Sermon on the Mount, Christ said: *"Blessed are the poor in spirit, for theirs is the kingdom of heaven. (Matt 5:3).* Christ referred to the blessing of being poor in spirit: the reward would be the kingdom of heaven.

Christ became poor for our sake, so that we might become rich.

For you know the grace of our Lord Jesus Christ, that though he was rich, yet for your sakes he became poor, so that you through his poverty might become rich. (2 Cor 8:9)

God has promised those, poor according to the world, that they would be rich in faith and inherit the kingdom of heaven.

Has not God chosen those who are poor in the eyes of the world to be rich in faith and to inherit the kingdom he promised those who love him? (James 2:5)

In any case, Christ has come to fulfill the prophecy of Isaiah and bring about restoration of those who are poor. Christ came to preach the gospel, the good news, to the poor—so that they would no longer be poor. The gospel of Christ is the message that no one can be poor who knows the love of God. The love of God makes everyone rich beyond measure.

Further, the Disciples of Christ and the Christian church are also to preach the gospel to those in need. We are to make the spiritually poor spiritually rich.

To preach good news to the poor (Luke 4:18)

Because of Love, He came …

Chapter 20. For the Son of Man came to seek and to save the lost. (Luke 19:10 RSV)

And Jesus said to him, "Today salvation has come to this house, since he also is a son of Abraham. **For the Son of Man came to seek and to save the lost**.*" (Luke 19:10 RSV)*

This reason for the Incarnation is to bring salvation to the lost.

Luke used an episode when Jesus was passing through Jericho in order to present this truth.

He [Jesus] entered Jericho and was passing through. And there was a man named Zacchaeus; he was a chief tax collector, and rich. And he sought to see who Jesus was, but could not, on account of the crowd, because he was small of stature. So he ran on ahead and climbed up into a sycamore tree to see him, for he was to pass that way. And when Jesus came to the place, he looked up and said to him, "Zacchaeus, make haste and come down; for I must stay at your house today." So he made haste and came down, and received him joyfully. And when they saw it they all murmured, "He has gone in to be the guest of a man who is a sinner." 8 And Zacchaeus stood and said to the Lord, "Behold, Lord, the half of my goods I give to the poor; and if I have defrauded any one of anything, I restore it fourfold." And Jesus said to him, "Today salvation has come to this house, since he also is a son of Abraham. For the Son of man came to seek and to save the lost." (Luke 19:1-10 RSV)

Luke's message is direct: *For the Son of Man came to seek and to save what was lost. (Luke 19:10 RSV)*

This story deals with a chief tax collector who was an outcast in Jewish society but not an outcast in God's society. To the Jews,

Zacchaeus was a *sinner;* to Christ, Zacchaeus was lost, but he was seeking Jesus Christ and the salvation that was only possible through Him.

No one in that crowd wanted to see Jesus more than Zacchaeus; no one in that crowd was as ready to repent as was Zacchaeus.

Zacchaeus was not to be denied.

Jesus Christ saw the heart of Zacchaeus differently than anyone else in that crowd. It was different because it was expectant; it was different because Zacchaeus had a high and noble understanding of just who Christ was. Zacchaeus also understood who he was.

We don't know the size of the crowd. We do know that that day, in Jericho, one sinner came home.

One sinner sought Christ: one sinner received salvation.

This passage brings up four subjects. The first is Zacchaeus, the *lost*; the second is Jesus Christ, the *Son of Man*; the third is to *seek;* the fourth is to *save*.

This is a message of evangelism: Jesus Christ came to call sinners to repentance. He came to *seek* and to *save*.

First, who is this Zacchaeus? Physically, he is short, small man. He is hated by his fellow Jews because he works for the despised Roman Empire as a chief tax-collector. He is an outcast in his own society. However, he knew that he was *lost*: he knew that he was a sinner in darkness. In addition, he was *seeking* to return to God.

He was lost, and he was seeking God. Christ seeks those who seek God: Christ saved those who seek Him. Christ identified Zacchaeus as *a son of Abraham.*

Second, who is this Son of Man who has come to seek and save the lost? This title, Son of Man, is used 86 times in the New Testament, beginning with Matthew 8:20 and concluding with Revelation 14:14.

I [the apostle John] looked, and there before me was a white cloud, and seated on the cloud was one "like a son of man" with a crown of gold on his head and a sharp sickle in his hand. (Rev 14:14)

Jesus used this title for Himself more than any other. It is likely that He did so because it was not associated with the Messiah or with any idea of restoration of the throne of David.

As such, Jesus applied this title to Himself in three ways.

First, He used the title in a general way, almost as a substitute for the pronoun *I*. An example is the statement that *the Son of Man has nowhere to lay His head (Luke 9:58)*. In this instance, He warned a would-be disciple that those who wanted to follow Him must share His earthly existence.

Second, Jesus used the title to emphasize that *the Son of Man must suffer (Mark 8:31)*, which implies that His suffering was foretold by the prophets. *Why then is it written that the Son of Man must suffer much and be rejected? But I tell you, Elijah has come, and they have done to him everything they wished, just as it is written about him. (Mark 9:12-13)*. At the Last Supper with His apostles, Jesus announced that He would be betrayed, *The Son of Man will go just as it is written about him. (Mark 14:21)*. Later on the same evening He submitted to His captors with the words: *Every day I was with you, teaching in the temple courts, and you did not arrest me. But the Scriptures must be fulfilled. Then everyone deserted him and fled. (Mark 14:49-50)*

Third, Jesus used the title, Son of Man, to reveal that He had divine authority in heaven and on earth, which was given to Him by His Father. *Then Jesus came to them and said, "All authority in heaven and on earth has been given to me." (Matt 28:18)*. In addition, Jesus said: *But that you may know that the Son of Man has authority on earth to forgive sins … (Mark 2:10)*. By claiming the authority to forgive sins, the Jews accused Jesus of blasphemy, by equating Himself with God. Jesus went one step further by claiming that the Son of Man was Lord of the Sabbath. *Then he said to them, "The Sabbath was made for man, not man for the Sabbath. So the Son of Man is Lord even of the Sabbath." (Mark 2:27-28)*

Further, Jesus spoke of His authority as the Son of Man at the end of time. *At that time men will see the Son of Man coming in clouds with great power and glory. (Mark 13:26)*. Jesus also declared to the high priest at His trial before His crucifixion: *Again the high priest asked him, "Are you the Christ, the Son of the Blessed One?" "I am," said Jesus. "And you will see the Son of Man sitting at the right hand of the Mighty One and coming on the clouds of heaven." (Mark 14:61-62)*. At the end of this age, the Son of Man will come on the clouds of heaven with great power and glory.

Such is the Son of Man who came to Jericho.

But the Son of Man came to *seek* and to *save*. That word, *seek*, needs no explanation; however, it is beneficial to understand what the Scriptures say about *God seeking* and *our seeking*.

For example, consider the following passages.

I [God] revealed myself to those who did not ask for me; I was found by those who did not seek me. To a nation that did not call on my name, I said, 'Here am I, here am I.' All day long I have held out my hands to an obstinate people, who walk in ways not good, pursuing their own imaginations — a people who continually provoke me to my very face, (Isa 65:1-3).

"For I [God] know the plans I have for you," declares the LORD, "plans to prosper you and not to harm you, plans to give you hope and a future. Then you will call upon me and come and pray to me, and I will listen to you. You will seek me and find me when you seek me with all your heart. I will be found by you," declares the LORD, (Jer 29:11-14).

"You will seek me [God] and find me when you seek me with all your heart. I will be found by you," declares the LORD," (Jer 29:13).

This is what the LORD says to the house of Israel: "Seek me and live;" (Amos 5:4).

God holds out His hands to those who seek Him; God loves those who love Him and those who seek Him find Him. We will find God when we seek Him with all of our heart; if we seek God, we will know His salvation.

Now, the Son of Man came also to *save* which consists of four terms: *justification, sanctification, edification, and glorification.*

Justification means that a repentant sinner has been tried in court, declared innocent, freed of the charge—all through the blood of Christ. Justification is the opposite of condemnation. *Sanctification* means that we become the righteousness of God through receiving Christ and believing in His name. *Edification* means that we become mature in Christ as we grow in faith. *Glorification* means that we will be glorified, even as Christ is glorified. *And those he predestined, he also called; those he called, he also justified; those he justified, he also glorified.* (Rom 8:30)

And so Luke described Zacchaeus; Luke identified Christ as the

Son of Man who had come to seek and to save the lost; Luke explained that reason for the Incarnation.

Jesus said to him [Zacchaeus], "Today salvation has come to this house, because this man, too, is a son of Abraham. For the Son of Man came to seek and to save what was lost." (Luke 19:10)

*For the Son of Man came to seek and to save
what was lost. (Luke 19:10 RSV)*

Because of Love, He came …

Chapter 21. who gave himself for our sins to deliver us from the present evil age (Gal 1:3 RSV)

Grace to you and peace from God the Father and our Lord Jesus Christ, who gave himself for our sins to deliver us from the present evil age, according to the will of our God and Father; to whom be the glory forever and ever. Amen. (Gal 1:3-5 RSV)

This Galatian passage identifies the truth that Christ gave Himself to deliver and rescue us from the present evil age.

In addition, this passage contains four important messages: *first*, grace and peace come from God; *second*, Christ gave Himself for our sins; *third*, His purpose was to deliver us from the present evil age; *fourth*, this was according to the will of God. Because of these acts, glory belongs to God forever and ever.

Jesus Christ is the great Deliverer, just as He is the great Redeemer and the great Advocate.

The Scriptures emphasize: Christ *gave* Himself for our sins. He did it willingly and in love. He set His face to the cross in obedience to the will of His Father.

We begin by recognizing that Christianity can rightly be considered a *rescue* ministry to deliver the righteous from this present evil age.

Certainly every age might well be considered to be *the present evil age*. Consider Paul's picture of evil in his age. (Romans 1:28-32 RSV)

And since they did not see fit to acknowledge God, God gave them up to a base mind and to improper conduct. They were filled with all manner of wickedness, evil, covetousness, malice. Full of envy, murder, strife, deceit, malignity, they are gossips, slanderers, haters of God, insolent, haughty, boastful, inventors of evil, disobedient to parents, foolish, faithless, heartless, ruthless. Though they know God's decree that those who do such things deserve to die, they not only do them but approve those who practice them.

God-haters are in this litany of wickedness. As such, God-haters must recognize that there is a God, so this person is not an agnostic or one who denies the existence or presence of God. A God-hater must also hate love and truth and peace and joy and all the attributes of God. There can be no sadder commentary on the character of mankind than to be a God-hater.

Consider other descriptions of the evil in the world.

During His earthly ministry, Christ described that generation as *evil and adulterous (Matt 16:4 RSV), faithless and perverse (Matt 17:17 RSV),* and *adulterous and sinful (Mark 8:38 RSV).*

The apostle Peter described his generation as *crooked (Acts 2:40 RSV).*

The apostle Paul described his generation as *crooked and perverse generation (Phil 2:15 RSV).*

Those generations were described as *evil, adulterous, faithless, perverse, sinful, and crooked.*

Other terms used elsewhere in the Scriptures include *depraved, unbelieving, wicked, and corrupt.*

Let us look at some of these terms.

Evil is any combination of forces and ideologies that opposes God and His work of righteousness in the world (Rom 7:8-19). The source of evil in the world is Satan. Evil also comes from the hearts of men (Mark 7:20-23 RSV), it does not come from God (James 1:13 RSV).

Wicked denotes a relationship with Satan, who is called *the wicked one.* Wickedness is the product of evil thoughts and evil purposes. Jesus points out the origin of all wrong: *For from within, out of men's hearts, come evil thoughts, sexual immorality, theft, murder, adultery, greed, malice, deceit, lewdness, envy, slander, arrogance and folly. All these evils come from inside and make a man 'unclean.' (Mark 7:21-23)*

Adulterous is willful sexual intercourse with someone other than one's spouse. Jesus expanded the meaning of adultery to include lust: *But I [Christ] tell you that anyone who looks at a woman lustfully has already committed adultery with her in his heart. (Matt 5:28 RSV)*

Unbelieving is the lack of faith and trust in God and His provision and protection. For example, unbelief will prevent individuals from receiving the benefits of a relationship with God. Consider the story of the boy possessed by an evil spirit. The father asked Jesus to help him. *And Jesus said to him, "If you can! All things are possible to him who believes." Immediately the father of the child cried out and said, "I believe; help my unbelief!." (Mark 9:23-24 RSV)*

Perverse describes people who are habitually disobedient and live a life of deceit and falsehood.

Sin is a violation of the law of God in thought, word, and actions. Sin is lawlessness (1 John 3:4). Sin is the evidence of the denial of the living God. The penalty for sin is death: *For the wages of sin is death, but the gift of God is eternal life in Christ Jesus our Lord. (Rom 6:23 RSV)*

Corrupt means moral depravity and moral corruption (Gen 6:11 RSV; Gal 6:8 RSV.) which leads to moral ruin and hopelessness, the second death. *For he who sows to his own flesh will from the flesh reap corruption; but he who sows to the Spirit will from the Spirit reap eternal life. (Gal 6:8 RSV)*

Crooked, a form of wickedness, defines dishonest and illegal acts. As stated in Psalm 125:5, God will banish evildoers who turn to *crooked ways. But those who turn aside upon their crooked ways the LORD will lead away with evildoers! (Ps 125:5 RSV)*

Salvation for the righteous will come through the wisdom of God. Wisdom will save the righteous from wicked men who walk in dark ways, who delight in evil, whose paths are crooked and who are devious in their ways.

Wisdom will deliver you from the way of evil, from men of perverted speech, who forsake the paths of uprightness to walk in the ways of darkness, who rejoice in doing evil and delight in the perverseness of evil; men whose paths are crooked, and who are devious in their ways. (Prov 2:12-15 RSV)

Depravity defines the consummate sinful nature of man. Man, by his very nature, is depraved. Only the cross can overcome the sin that fills the hearts of such men.

All of those terms summarize the evil in every age. The world has changed little in terms of the evil which it breeds, which it commits, and which it tolerates.

However, Christianity, existing in the midst of evil, is to be the light of world and the salt of the earth. Christians are called to be different and to make a difference. We are not to do what they do. They do this; we are not to do evil.

They [the Israelites] despised his [God's] statutes, and his covenant that he made with their fathers, and the warnings which he gave them. They went after false idols, and became false, and they followed the nations that were round about them, concerning whom the LORD had commanded them that they should not do like them. (2 Kings 17:15 RSV)

Then said Jesus to the crowds and to his disciples, "The scribes and the Pharisees sit on Moses' seat; so practice and observe whatever they tell you, but not what they do; for they preach, but do not practice. (Matt 23:1-3 RSV)

Why do you call me, 'Lord, Lord,' and do not do what I say?' (Luke 6:46 RSV)

God has delivered us from the present evil age through His Son and the truths revealed through the Spirit.

*who gave himself for our sins to deliver us from
the present evil age (Gal 1:3 RSV)*

Because of Love, He came …

Chapter 22. It is for freedom that Christ has set us free (Gal 5:1)

It is for freedom that Christ has set us free. *Stand firm, then, and do not let yourselves be burdened again by a yoke of slavery. (Gal 5:1)*

He has sent me to bind up the brokenhearted, to proclaim freedom for the captives and release from darkness for the prisoners, (Isa 61:1)

Now the Lord is the Spirit, and where the Spirit of the Lord is, there is freedom. And we, who with unveiled faces all reflect the Lord's glory, are being transformed into his likeness with ever-increasing glory, which comes from the Lord, who is the Spirit. (2 Cor 3:17-18)

Christ came to set us free; that is a direct reason for the Incarnation.

Such an act on His part implies that we were in slavery to something, most likely sin, and to the things of this world. We needed to be set free: therefore, God sent His Son for that very purpose.

But what constitutes freedom? And what is the freedom that Christ came to give us?

Freedom has both a spiritual dimension and a physical dimension. The physical dimension is that condition in which we are physically restrained from doing what we might seek to do. The spiritual dimension deals with the choices and decisions that we make in a manner which is unrestrained and is consistent with the will of God.

In the context of this passage, the apostle Paul is talking about spiritual freedom. He is talking about the choice: either accepting God or the things of this world. He is talking about a life of sin or a life ruled by the love of God. He is talking about the things of the Spirit and the things of the flesh. He is talking about the difference between the truth and the lie.

In one way, Psalm 1 is indicative of the situation discussed here. In that Psalm, the choice is between two types of men: first, the righteous man who does not walk in the counsel of the wicked or stand in the way of sinners or sit in the seat of mockers: second, the wicked man who is a sinner and who mocks God. The righteous person delights in the law of the LORD, and he meditates day and night on God's law. Therefore, whatever he does prospers. Not so the wicked! As a result, the wicked will not stand in the judgment or sinners in the assembly of the righteous. For the Lord God watches over the way of the righteous, but the way of the wicked will perish.

There are choices to be made and decisions to be reached. However, the purpose of the Scriptures and the purpose of God is that we would make choices consistent with the will of God. Freedom means that we can exercise our will either in agreement with the will of God or contrary to the will of God. Therefore, we can choose to accept or reject God; we can choose to accept or reject Christ.

However, the Scriptures makes it clear that true freedom is found only in a relationship with God through His Son, Jesus Christ, and by the power of the Holy Spirit.

Consider three passages which relate to the concept of Christian freedom and which are consistent with the message that Christ came to set us free.

In John 8:31-32, we find this message: *To the Jews who had believed him, Jesus said, "If you hold to my teaching, you are really my disciples. Then you will know the truth, and the truth will set you free." (John 8:31-32)*

Jesus is making a remarkable statement here. He said: if you accept my teaching, two things will happen: first, that is the evidence that you really are my disciple; second, my teachings will proclaim the truth—and the truth in my teaching will set you free. Freedom is found in the acceptance of the teachings of Jesus Christ.

Next, consider the theology of the apostle Paul: *Now the Lord is the Spirit, and where the Spirit of the Lord is, there is freedom. And we, who with unveiled faces all reflect the Lord's glory, are being transformed into his likeness with ever-increasing glory, which comes from the Lord, who is the Spirit. (2 Cor 3:17-18)*

Paul has discovered that, where the Spirit of the Lord is, there is freedom. Conversely, where the Spirit is not present, there is no freedom. Therefore, freedom is related to the presence of the Spirit of God. This freedom results in our transformation into His likeness. Consider the benefits and value of freedom.

But the man who looks intently into the perfect law that gives freedom, and continues to do this, not forgetting what he has heard, but doing it — he will be blessed in what he does. (James 1:25)

The third passage (James 1:25) states that the perfect law, which is the law of God, gives freedom. Anyone who lives by that law will be blessed in what he does. The perfect law of God stands in sharp contrast to the imperfect law of sin (Rom 7:25).

Perfect is that which is without flaw or error; perfect is a state of completion or final fulfillment.

God is perfect, which means that He is complete in Himself. He is perfect in all the characteristics of His nature. He is the basis for and standard by which all other perfection is to be measured (Job 36:4; Ps 18:30; 19:7; Matt 5:48). Man, in his current state, is not perfect. Man may grow in maturity, but perfection is an eschatological concept which is related to the glorification of each believer in Christ as the final act of salvation.

So Christians have freedom. The Source of that freedom is the Cross of Christ. On the cross, Christ took on our sins and gave us freedom to be the righteousness of God.

His death procured our freedom. Christ, in turn, was set free from death by the resurrection which came from God alone. He was raised; God, through His Son, showed the evidence of victory over life and death.

As He was raised from the dead, so shall we know the same resurrection as Christ knew.

I [Paul] want to know Christ and the power of his resurrection and the fellowship of sharing in his sufferings, becoming like him in his death, and so, somehow, to attain to the resurrection from the dead. (Phil 3:10-11)

Christ has come to set us free from the bondage of slavery to sin. Therefore, we are to stand firm in that freedom which He has secured for us on the Cross. *It is for freedom that Christ has set us free. Stand firm, then, and do not let yourselves be burdened again by a yoke of slavery. (Gal 5:1)*

Jesus told the Jews that the *truth* will set you free. *To the Jews who had believed him, Jesus said, "If you hold to my teaching, you are really my disciples. Then you will know the truth, and the truth will set you free. (John 8:31-32)* Then Jesus told them that He, Jesus Christ, is the *Truth.* Christ is the Truth that will set us free. *Jesus answered, "I am the way and the truth and the life. No one comes to the Father except through me." (John 14:6)*

Final freedom will lead to the perfection of the New Creation. When there is the New Heaven and the New Earth and the New Jerusalem (Rev 21:1-4), then, and only then, will there be the total freedom which we will receive.

The cross gives freedom to all who receive the Lord Jesus Christ as Savior and Lord. The cross gave us Christ's righteousness as well as releasing us from the sinful nature that demonizes a person and prevents union with God.

The Cross of Christ is the only door to redemption and reconciliation with God; the Cross of Christ is the only door to true spiritual freedom.

Paul explained the freedom for which Christ died and which we receive as a result of His death. Paul reminded the world that this freedom is found in faith, not in the law. Paul further stressed that the only thing that counts is faith expressed through love; it is love for God and love for each other (Deut 6:5; Lev 19:18). Our love for God is *because he first loved us. (1 John 4:19)* We would not know love unless we know God. God is love, and His love is the perfect example of freedom. Love leads to faith; faith is having assurance and confidence in God. Further, faith is the total acceptance of the Person of Christ as Redeemer and Lord; it is also the total acceptance of the saving work of Christ for our redemption and reconciliation with God.

The gospel of Christ is the message of freedom in Christ. When we die to the old self, we become the new man in Christ who now lives in the fullness of freedom.

There is perfect love in freedom; there is perfect faith in freedom. Faith leads to freedom; increased freedom leads to an increased faith.

There is no freedom apart from a divine relationship with God. God is freedom; God is the Source of freedom for His people. God sent His Son, the Christ, to set us free. The freedom that Christ has provided us is a redeemed and reconciled relationship with God. Sin no longer has dominion over us. The dominion we now enjoy is that under the Lordship of Jesus Christ with the freedom to love and serve God.

It is the freedom to have Christ formed in us; it is freedom to have Christ live in us.

It is the freedom to be open to the Spirit of God so that the fruit of the Spirit will be evident in our lives.

It is the freedom to accept the truths of God and the freedom to reject the lies of the devil.

It is the freedom to walk is the Spirit and to be led by the Spirit.

When we belong to Christ, then we know the fullness of freedom.

It is the freedom to become a new creation when we accept the freedom that comes through Christ.

God had also called those in slavery to become free men so that they can become Christ's slave. *Were you a slave when you were called? Don't let it trouble you — although if you can gain your freedom, do so. For he who was a slave when he was called by the Lord is the Lord's freedman; similarly, he who was a free man when he was called is Christ's slave. (1 Cor 7:21-23)*

Christ on the cross has freed us from the dominion of sin. We, once in darkness to sin, have now been brought into the glorious light of the Son of God; we now experience the freedom which can only come through love and faith in Christ Jesus. Freed from the burden and dominion of sin, Christ has set our feet on the pathway to righteousness.

Therefore, Christian freedom means thinking and acting in a manner which brings glory to God. Freedom begins with discernment and relies upon the Holy Spirit to do those things which are true representations of Christian freedom. Christian freedom leads to Christian action. Christian freedom is a witness to the love that God has showered upon us and the responsive love that we have for God, for the Incarnation, for the gospel, for the Kingdom of God, and for eternal life.

Freedom requires thanksgiving to God. Just as faith without works is dead, so is freedom without gratitude to God who makes all true freedom possible.

Freedom is found in Christ because the basis for freedom is the Cross of Christ.

There are several truths that relate to freedom. First, Jesus Christ quoted from Isa 61:1 when He spoke in the synagogue in Nazareth that God had anointed Him to preach good news (the gospel) to the poor. God had sent Christ to proclaim *freedom* for the prisoners, recovery of sight for the blind, and for the release of the oppressed. Christ is speaking both spiritually and physically.

The Spirit of the Lord is on me [Christ], because he has anointed me to preach good news to the poor. He has sent me to proclaim freedom for the prisoners and recovery of sight for the blind, to release the oppressed, to proclaim the year of the Lord's favor. (Luke 4:18-19; Isa 61:1-2)

Christ said: I am the truth—and the truth shall set you free.

Christ, as the Truth, has set us free; there is no freedom except that found in a loving and committed relationship with Christ.

And so Paul encourages the world to seek the freedom which is found only by faith in Jesus Christ. We are called to be a new people. We are to be free of sin; we are to stand firm in faith to the Lord God.

By His Incarnation, Christ, the Truth, has set us free.

It is for freedom that Christ has set us free (Gal 5:1)

Because of Love, He came …

Chapter 23. This, then, is how you should pray (Matt 6:9)

But when you pray, go into your room, close the door and pray to your Father, who is unseen. Then your Father, who sees what is done in secret, will reward you. And when you pray, do not keep on babbling like pagans, for they think they will be heard because of their many words. Do not be like them, for your Father knows what you need before you ask him. **This, then, is how you should pray**: *"Our Father in heaven, hallowed be your name, your kingdom come, your will be done on earth as it is in heaven. Give us today our daily bread. Forgive us our debts, as we also have forgiven our debtors. And lead us not into temptation, but deliver us from the evil one." (Matt 6:6-13)*

So I [Christ] say to you: Ask and it will be given to you; seek and you will find; knock and the door will be opened to you. 10 For everyone who asks receives; he who seeks finds; and to him who knocks, the door will be opened. (Luke 11:9-10)

Prayer is the evidence of a divine relationship with God. Therefore, Christ came so that we would know something of the relationship that He shared with God the Father.

Prayer is a divine conversation *with* the Father. We don't pray *to* God; we pray *with* God. Prayer is a time of speaking but also a time of listening. The more important time in prayer is when God speaks to us.

That divine conversation was the result of the Disciples' request to Christ: *Lord, teach us to pray. (Luke 11:1)*

It is interesting that the disciples could have asked Jesus to teach them any one of a number of things, e.g. how to proclaim the Kingdom of God, how to teach, how to heal the sick, how to increase faith, etc.

But they didn't. They asked this one thing: *Lord, teach us to pray (Luke 11:1).* Why?

It was because the disciples saw the power in prayer. They saw that prayer was an expression of the unity of the Father and the Son. They saw that Christ found love and power and peace in prayer. They saw that prayer would the first option before Christ did anything. If it was this important to Him, then they wanted to know and experience the same relationship and the same peace and power that He had received through prayer.

Prayer unites us with God: that is divine peace.

They saw the Son speak with the Father; they saw the results of those divine conversations. They saw the power and the resolve and the confidence that comes only from a relationship with God in which the will of God is expressed and fulfilled.

Although the disciples did not realize the fullness of what occurred, they knew that something powerful and significant had resulted.

They saw Him pray in every situation: from feeding the 5,000 to the time of facing the cross. Prayer is the battleground: when the praying is completed and the will of God is understood, then the victory is won.

Only after prayer with God will we be equipped to face whatever lay ahead.

The disciples saw Him turn to the Father. Consider just two occasions: first, the feeding of the 5,000 in Matthew 14; second, the great priestly prayer in John 17.

And he [Christ] directed the people to sit down on the grass. Taking the five loaves and the two fish and looking up to heaven, he gave thanks and broke the loaves. Then he gave them to the disciples, and the disciples gave them to the people. (Matt 14:19)

After Jesus said this, he looked toward heaven and prayed: "Father, the time has come. Glorify your Son, that your Son may glorify you. (John 17:1)

In these two passages, Christ was *looking up to heaven,* and He *looked toward heaven.* This *looking* was both a physical and a spiritual act. Since these two words, God and heaven, are interchangeable, when Christ looked toward heaven, He looked toward God.

In the same manner, when we pray, we are to look to God; we do so to seek the Face of God. We do so to know the will of God; we do so to fulfill the will of God.

We look toward God because that is the Source of omnipotence and omniscience. All things are possible through God.

Therefore, one of the reasons for the birth of Christ was to demonstrate the power of prayer in the lives of every believer—but also to give believers a model for prayer (Matt 6:9-13 and Luke 11:2-4).

Christ said: pray to *our Father*. We first recognize this as a corporate prayer; notice that all the pronouns are plural. Second, recognize how we are to pray: *first, God*: give glory to the Father; seek for His Kingdom to come; seek for His will on earth; *second, us*: seek His forgiveness of our sins; seek for God to lead us through temptation; seek for God to protect us from Satan; *third*, return to God, acknowledging His kingdom, His power and His glory.

It is a simple prayer and one which is a model for our conversation with God. We are to speak *with* God from our hearts and from the situation at that time.

Jesus Christ, the Model of prayer, came to teach those who believe in Him how and when to pray.

If you believe, you will receive whatever you ask for in prayer. (Matt 21:22)

Paul, also a model of prayer, taught the same consistent truths as Christ.

Be joyful in hope, patient in affliction, faithful in prayer. (Rom 12:12-13)

One of the great admonitions of the Scriptures is that we should *rejoice always, pray constantly*. These four words provide a platform for the Christian life.

Be joyful always; pray continually; give thanks in all circumstances, for this is God's will for you in Christ Jesus. (1 Thess 5:16-18)

Since God is our Father, it naturally follows that we will be His children.

It also naturally follows that loving children would seek to speak with their Father. It raises the question: if children never speak to their

Father, what kind of relationship would that be? It follows that those children who seek a loving relationship with their Father would seek to speak *with* Him regularly. Further, speaking with our Father implies that we would seek what He would tell us and teach us.

It is clear that God, our Father, would have much more to tell us than we have to tell Him.

Therefore, as children, we are to have divine conversations with our Father: that is the purpose of prayer.

Notice also that our prayers are Trinitarian. That is, we pray to the Father in the power of the Spirit and in the name of the Son.

Notice also that Jesus has told us that, if we ask, we will receive. If we seek, we will find. If we knock, the door will be opened.

Ask and it will be given to you; seek and you will find; knock and the door will be opened to you. For everyone who asks receives; he who seeks finds; and to him who knocks, the door will be opened. (Matt 7:7-8)

Jesus said: a*sk, seek,* and *knock.*

Jesus also said that if you ask anything in His name, He will do it.

And I will do whatever you ask in my name, so that the Son may bring glory to the Father. You may ask me for anything in my name, and I will do it. (John 14:13-14)

A further dimension of prayer is that we should seek the leading of the Spirit to guide us in our prayer life. The Apostle Paul reminds us that the Spirit will help us in our weakness and show us how we should pray.

In the same way, the Spirit helps us in our weakness. We do not know what we ought to pray for, but the Spirit himself intercedes for us with groans that words cannot express. And he who searches our hearts knows the mind of the Spirit, because the Spirit intercedes for the saints in accordance with God's will. And we know that in all things God works for the good of those who love him, who have been called according to his purpose. (Rom 8:26-28)

Prayer, our divine conversation with God, is not something we do only when we are in church or when we are preparing for meals. We should pray constantly: when we are walking, when we are sitting, when we are playing golf, when we are looking up to heaven, or at any time.

We should always seek to be one with our Father. We seek Him, His will, and His glory. That is why we pray.

This message is emphasized in 2 Chronicles 7:14.

If my people who are called by my name humble themselves, and pray and seek my face, and turn from their wicked ways, then I will hear from heaven, and will forgive their sin and heal their land. (2 Chron 7:14 RSV)

Several of the great promises of the Scriptures are contained in 2 Chron 7:14. If we are humble, pray, seek the face of God, and turn from our wicked ways, then God promises to hear from heaven, forgive our sin and heal our land.

Everyone faces a share of difficult moments and difficult situations. When they arise, we must first seek the Face of God. We should not first seek the advice of friends. This truth is clear: prayer is not our last option: God is not our last option. No, God must be our first option: prayer must be our first option.

Let me add a word about our posture in prayer. Some kneel and bow their heads; that is fine. Some stand erect and look up to heaven to seek the face of God. There are no physical regulations regarding prayer. No, what is important is the condition of the heart. Is our heart humble before the Lord God? Do we love and honor the One to whom we turn? It is our spiritual posture, not our physical posture that we should be concerned about. In prayer, we spiritually kneel before our Father in heaven.

In every situation, the first thing that Christ did was pray. He sought the Presence of His Father and the power of His Presence which came from prayer.

I [Christ] pray for them. I am not praying for the world, but for those you have given me, for they are yours. (John 17:9)

However, prayer is not solely about us and our needs. Prayer is about God, His will and His purpose. Prayer is about our neighbors and our enemies.

You have heard that it was said, 'Love your neighbor and hate your enemy.' But I [Christ] tell you: Love your enemies and pray for those who persecute you, that you may be sons of your Father in heaven. He causes his sun to rise on the evil and the good, and sends rain on the righteous and the unrighteous. (Matt 5:43-45)

In every situation, the key is to fix our eyes on Jesus: *Therefore, since we are surrounded by such a great cloud of witnesses, let us throw off everything that hinders and the sin that so easily entangles, and let us run with perseverance the race marked out for us. Let us fix our eyes on Jesus, the author and perfecter of our faith, who for the joy set before him endured the cross, scorning its shame, and sat down at the right hand of the throne of God. Consider him who endured such opposition from sinful men, so that you will not grow weary and lose heart. In your struggle against sin, you have not yet resisted to the point of shedding your blood.* (Heb 12:1-4)

Finally, Christians should pray: not that we would be safe in this world but that we would be faithful.

Christ is the example of prayer; when we know Him, we shall know the power of prayer.

The Incarnation was to show us the close relationship between the Father and the Son that was evident in His praying. That relationship can be ours when Christ lives in us and we in Him.

This, then, is how you should pray (Matt 6:9)

Because of Love, He came …

Chapter 24. If you hold to my teaching, you are really my disciples (John 8:31)

*To the Jews who had believed him, Jesus said, "**If you hold to my teaching, you are really my disciples**. Then you will know the truth, and the truth will set you free." (John 8:31-32)*

A new command I give you: Love one another. As I have loved you, so you must love one another. By this all men will know that you are my disciples, if you love one another. (John 13:34-35)

If you remain in me and my words remain in you, ask whatever you wish, and it will be given you. This is to my Father's glory, that you bear much fruit, showing yourselves to be my disciples. (John 15:7-8)

The Incarnation led to the choosing and teaching His disciples so that they would continue the ministry which Christ had begun. Christ was seeking those who would hold to His teaching, which means that they would be faithful in both the understanding and the proclamation of all that He had taught them.

Continuation of His teaching was essential; trustworthy and faithful disciples were essential for that purpose.

Christ came to proclaim the gospel and to advance the Kingdom of God; His disciples were to continue those teachings. To do so, Christ chose disciples who would fulfill the responsibility that He would give them.

The major difficulty was to ensure that His teachings would not be corrupted by false teachers who might choose to insert into His message teachings which Christ did not sanction. For example, the

Judaizers were false teachers who would add circumcision and the Law to the gospel of Christ. This is the very issue which the Apostle Paul attacked and condemned in his Epistle to the Galatians.

In His final command to His disciples, Christ told His disciples to *teach them to obey everything I have commanded you.*

Then Jesus came to them and said, "All authority in heaven and on earth has been given to me. Therefore go and make disciples of all nations, baptizing them in the name of the Father and of the Son and of the Holy Spirit, and teaching them to obey everything I have commanded you. And surely I am with you always, to the very end of the age." (Matt 28:18-20)

All authority has been given to Christ; we are to serve under His authority and make disciples of all nations; we are to baptize them; we are to teach all that He has taught us. If we are faithful in this responsibility, Christ has promised to be with us, *to the very end of the age.*

What Christ commanded then is what Christ commands today.

The call to being a disciple was both an invitation and a promise. The invitation is to obedience and faithfulness to the will of God and to His Son; the promise is that *God has said, "Never will I leave you; never will I forsake you." (Heb 13:5)*

In addition, His disciples were to be His witnesses in all the world.

But you will receive power when the Holy Spirit comes on you; and you will be my witnesses in Jerusalem, and in all Judea and Samaria, and to the ends of the earth. (Acts 1:8)

However, the hallmark of a disciple of Christ is that he would be a witness to Christ by faithfulness to the teachings of Christ.

With these credentials, they were to go and make disciples of all nations who would be equally faithful to the divine teachings of Christ.

But what is the definition and character of a disciple?

In general, a disciple was a student under a master or teacher. To be a disciple meant following faithfully the teachings of that particular master. In addition, the student would leave the teacher after a certain period of time and go out on his own, teaching much of what he had learned. Is such cases, there was no lasting relationship between the teacher and the student. A disciple is also considered one who professed to have learned certain principles from another and maintains them on that other's authority. In the widest sense, it refers to those who accept the teachings of anyone, not only in belief but in life.

However, with Jesus, the process was entirely different. He did not seek volunteers: He called men with divine authority, in the same way that God called His prophets in the Old Testament. Further, with Jesus, there was to be a permanent and lasting relationship between the master and his student. With Jesus, the entire life of the disciple was directed in love, faithfulness, obedience, and service.

Also with Jesus, the term, disciple, implied a spiritual relationship. Jesus was dealing with both the spiritual and the physical: however, He emphasized more the spiritual content of His teachings.

Those who were called as disciples were also called to share in Jesus' authority. In addition, they will sit with Him on thrones in the judgment of the world (Matt 19:28; Luke 22:30).

Jesus said to them, "I tell you the truth, at the renewal of all things, when the Son of Man sits on his glorious throne, you who have followed me will also sit on twelve thrones, judging the twelve tribes of Israel. And everyone who has left houses or brothers or sisters or father or mother or children or fields for my sake will receive a hundred times as much and will inherit eternal life. But many who are first will be last, and many who are last will be first." (Matt 19:28-30).

Christ now defined the qualifications of those who are to be His disciples.

To begin with, a disciple must expect the same treatment and rejection as Christ received; therefore suffering and persecution are a part of discipleship.

Blessed are those who are persecuted because of righteousness, for theirs is the kingdom of heaven. Blessed are you when people insult you, persecute you and falsely say all kinds of evil against you because of me. Rejoice and be glad, because great is your reward in heaven, for in the same way they persecuted the prophets who were before you. (Matt 5:10-12)

However, Christ said that His disciples will be blessed by the persecution that they endure, for *great is your reward in heaven.*

Further, Christ said: *anyone who does not take his cross and follow me is not worthy of me. (Matt 10:38)* Christ also said that His disciples must take up his cross daily and follow Him. If we are crucified with Christ, then Christ lives in us and we live in Him (Gal 2:20).

Above all, Christ makes the condition for discipleship clear: His disciples must be faithful to His teachings. That is fundamental. In like manner, their teaching must be faithful to Christ's, regardless of any rejection and persecution that might arise.

So, what basically did Jesus teach? The Sermon on the Mount is a primary example: in those passages, Christ taught three basic subjects: *first*, a broader love; *second*, a deeper righteousness; *third*, a nobler ambition.

A broader love: to love those who love you and to love your enemies. *But I tell you: Love your enemies and pray for those who persecute you, that you may be sons of your Father in heaven. (Matt 5:44-45)*

A deeper righteousness: beyond the law with righteousness based on grace and truth: *For I tell you that unless your righteousness surpasses that of the Pharisees and the teachers of the law, you will certainly not enter the kingdom of heaven. (Matt 5:20)*

A nobler ambition: to seek the things of God and not the things of this world: *But seek first his kingdom and his righteousness, and all these things will be given to you as well. (Matt 6:33)*

In addition, He taught about the gospel and Kingdom of God which were His primary subjects throughout His earthly ministry.

He began His earthly ministry with these words: *Repent, for the kingdom of heaven is near. (Matt 4:17)*

Jesus pointed them to the future dawn of the Kingdom of God. *He said to another man, "Follow me." But the man replied, "Lord, first let me go and bury my father." Jesus said to him, "Let the dead bury their own dead, but you go and proclaim the kingdom of God." Still another said, "I will follow you, Lord; but first let me go back and say good-by to my family." Jesus replied, "No one who puts his hand to the plow and looks back is fit for service in the kingdom of God." (Luke 9:59-62)*

Jesus taught His disciples all that was necessary for love and service in the Kingdom of God.

In addition, Jesus appears as a Light and Life in the world of darkness and death. Anyone who follows Him walks in the light and is saved (John 8:12). Christ taught that His disciples were to follow Him and serve Him. To follow Christ means that the Father will honor those who serve the Son.

Whoever serves me must follow me; and where I am, my servant also will be. My Father will honor the one who serves me. (John 12:26)

In all cases, a disciple of Jesus Christ must be faithful to His teachings, must love one another, must bear much fruit, must love Christ more than our earthly family, must take up our cross and follow Him, to know that we are called to lose our life for His sake, and to give up everything we have, all physical possessions and all earthly relationships—for spiritual riches.

Being a disciple of Christ is best summarized in John 15, where Christ said: I am the Vine and you are the branches.

I [Christ] am the true vine, and my Father is the gardener. He cuts off every branch in me that bears no fruit, while every branch that does bear fruit he prunes so that it will be even more fruitful … Remain in me, and I will remain in you. No branch can bear fruit by itself; it must remain in the vine. Neither can you bear fruit unless you remain in me. "I am the vine; you are the branches. If a man remains in me and I in him, he will bear much fruit; apart from me you can do nothing … If you remain in me and my words remain in you, ask whatever you wish, and it will be given you. This is to my Father's glory, that you bear much fruit, showing yourselves to be my disciples. (John 15:1-8)

Note the character of the disciple as defined by Christ in this passage.

The Son is the true vine; the Father is the true gardener.

The Father cuts off every branch that bears no fruit, while every branch that does bear fruit he prunes so that it will be even more fruitful. Recognize this truth: Christ *produces* the fruit; we *bear* the fruit.

Jesus said to His disciples: *remain in me, and I will remain in you.* Christ and His disciples are to be permanently and eternally attached.

The purpose of that eternal relationship is so that the branches will bear the fruit by itself, produced by the Vine. His disciples cannot bear fruit unless they remain in Christ. Christ is the vine; we are the branches. If we remain in Christ and He remains in us, we will bear much fruit. The truth is this: apart from Christ, we can do nothing.

The ultimate truth is this: if we bear much fruit, there are two results: *first*, God is glorified; *second*, we show the world that we are Christ's disciples.

The conditions for being a disciple of Christ's then are identical to the conditions of being a disciple today.

Christ came into the world to choose those whom He would trust with the message of the gospel and the Kingdom of God and to make disciples of all nations.

If you hold to my teaching, you are really my disciples (John 8:32)

Because of Love, He came …

Chapter 25. if anyone is in Christ, he is a new creation (2 Cor 5:17 RSV)

Therefore, if anyone is in Christ, he is a new creation; the old has passed away, behold, the new has come. All this is from God, who through Christ reconciled us to himself and gave us the ministry of reconciliation; that is, in Christ God was reconciling the world to himself, not counting their trespasses against them, and entrusting to us the message of reconciliation. So we are ambassadors for Christ, God making his appeal through us. We beseech you on behalf of Christ, be reconciled to God. For our sake he made him to be sin who knew no sin, so that in him we might become the righteousness of God. (2 Cor 5:17-21 RSV)

But far be it from me to glory except in the cross of our Lord Jesus Christ, by which the world has been crucified to me, and I to the world. For neither circumcision counts for anything, nor uncircumcision, but a new creation. (Gal 6:14-15 RSV)

We now address the concept of the new creation which is a divine transformation, resulting from being in Christ and through the leading of the Holy Spirit.

As we shall see, the Incarnation is basic to becoming a new creation. Without the earthly ministry of Christ, there can be no new creation, for to be a new creation demands that we be *in Christ*.

God, the Creator, is faithful to His eternal plan to make His created into His image. To do so requires that we become a new creation. God has chosen to make us *new*. That means that the *old self* has died and that the *new man* is one totally different in love, in faith, in freedom, in understanding, in vision, and in action. This is not a modified *old man*; this is a new person, with a new perspective, with a new understanding of God, with a new appreciation for Christ and His cross, with a new understanding of the power of the Spirit, with a new understanding of the power of prayer, with a new vision of our role as the light of the world and the salt of the earth, with a new understanding of the Kingdom of God, and with a new understanding of our responsibility to evangelize the world with the gospel of God. All things become new; the new person sees the same old world in a new light. The darkness is removed; the Light of the world has come into the world. It is God's creation; it is God's world; it is His kingdom, under the Lordship of His Son, Jesus Christ.

Paul introduced this concept of a *new creation* in his Epistle to the Galatians, where his argument is this: salvation is through faith alone in Christ alone; no one comes to the Father except through the Son. Justification is by faith in Christ: freedom in Christ is the result of faith in Christ. Paul concluded this epistle with eight truths: *first,* live so as to fulfill the *law of Christ*; *second,* live so as to develop your Christian character; *third,* honor those who teach you godly truths; *fourth,* have a noble vision of God; *fifth,* know that you will reap what you sow; *sixth,* have a strong relationship with all members of the community of faith; *seventh*; discern the truth; stand firm in faith against those who corrupt the truth; *eighth,* become a *new creation* in Christ.

Paul was later to expand this meaning of the *new creation* (Ephesians 2:11-18) by stating that Christ on the cross created for Himself a *new man* who is to be redeemed and reconciled to God.

The *new creation* is identical with the *new man*.

Therefore remember that at one time you Gentiles in the flesh, called the uncircumcision by what is called the circumcision, which is made in the flesh by hands - remember that you were at that time separated from Christ, alienated from the commonwealth of Israel, and strangers to the covenants of promise, having no hope and without God in the world. But now in Christ Jesus you who once were far off have been brought near in the blood of Christ. For he is our peace, who has made us both one, and has broken down the dividing wall of hostility, by abolishing in his flesh the law of commandments and ordinances, that he might create in himself one new man in place of the two, so making peace, and might reconcile us

*both to God in one body through the cross, thereby bringing the hostility
to an end. And he came and preached peace to you who were far off and
peace to those who were near; for through him we both have access in
one Spirit to the Father. (Eph 2:11-18 RSV)*

This passage reflects the gospel of Christ. It defines the state of
man: *separate from Christ, excluded from citizenship … foreigners to the
covenants of the promise, without hope and without God in the world.* But
Christ has come to make the two one, by making the *circumcised* and
the *uncircumcised* one, thereby creating *one new man, making peace,*
and *in this one united body to reconcile both of them to God through the
cross, by which he put to death their hostility.* On the cross, Christ put to
death the hostility that existed between the circumcised (Jews) and
the uncircumcised (pagans).

In this passage, Paul identified an additional great truth regarding
the cross. The cross not only provided forgiveness of sins for those who
receive and believe in Him; the cross also provided for the *abolishing in
his [Christ's] flesh the law with its commandments and regulations.*

Hostility is shown in sin. When sin is removed, hostility is removed.
Unity, through redemption and reconciliation, is the result.

Paul said: the only thing in which anyone can boast is the Cross
of Christ. We *boast* about the cross because it is the means by which
Christ has redeemed and reconciled us to God. The cross is the call to
salvation: the cross is the bridge that unites us with God and to our
fellow believers.

Paul concluded that we become a *new creation* through the Cross
of Christ.

Paul later expanded this concept of the *new creation* in 2
Corinthians 5:17 RSV.

Being a *new creation* is the result of being *in Christ.* Since both
concepts, new creation and being in Christ, are central to the gospel,
it is essential that we understand what it means to be *in Christ* and to
being a *new creation.* Anyone who is *in Christ* will be a *new creation.* The
two concepts, being *in Christ* and being a *new creation,* are inseparable.

• *in Christ*

To understand what it means to be *in Christ,* we shall first state

140

what it is not. It does not mean that Christ is like a box, and we are in the box. That is not the sense of being *in Christ*.

The fullness of the meaning of this term, *in Christ*, comes from an understanding of two passages: Matthew 11:28-30 RSV and John 15:5-8 RSV.

Come to me [Christ], all who labor and are heavy laden, and I will give you rest. Take my yoke upon you, and learn from me; for I am gentle and lowly in heart, and you will find rest for your souls. For my yoke is easy, and my burden is light. (Matt 11:28-30 RSV)

I am the vine, you are the branches. He who abides in me, and I in him, he it is that bears much fruit, for apart from me you can do nothing. If a man does not abide in me, he is cast forth as a branch and withers; and the branches are gathered, thrown into the fire and burned. If you abide in me, and my words abide in you, ask whatever you will, and it shall be done for you. By this my Father is glorified, that you bear much fruit, and so prove to be my disciples. (John 15:5-8 RSV)

These two passages present the companion thought of being *yoked with Christ* as well as being the *branch attached to the Vine*.

We are considered *in Christ* when we are *yoked* with Him; similarly, we are *in Christ* when we are the *branches* attached to the *Vine*. As a yoke, we are forever united with Him; as a branch, we are always attached to Him.

Let us look more carefully at these two ideas.

The first one: to be *yoked with Christ* is to be understood in a spiritual sense, not in a physical sense. Notice carefully that to be yoked with Christ is that we would find *rest for our souls*. Now a yoke is a type of harness which connected a pair of animals to a plow; a yoke is used to link them together so they could work efficiently. In a symbolic sense, the term, yoke, is used to describe the burden or oppression of heavy responsibility, duty, sin, or punishment (1 Kings 12:4-14; Jer 27:8-12; Acts 15:10). During the life of Jesus, the term, yoke, was used by the Jewish rabbis to mean: *to become the pupil of a certain teacher.* Jesus gave this invitation to His disciples: *Take My yoke upon you and learn from Me, for I am gentle and lowly in heart, and you will find rest for your souls. For My yoke is easy and My burden is light (Matt 11:29-30 RSV).*

Now, in the second passage, our relationship with Christ is

identified as that of the vine and the branch. In the Old Testament, the term, *branch*, is a symbolic title for the Messiah. This messianic term originated with the prophet Isaiah (4:2; 11:1), and it reappeared in the prophecies of Jeremiah, where it referred to a future king in the line of David, whose coming would bring judgment and righteousness (Jer 23:5-6). After the Captivity, the term, *branch*, was a recognized title of the Messiah (Zech 3:8). In the time of Zechariah, the term took on a priestly, as well as a kingly, meaning. The meaning of the branch represented the symbol of kings, as descended from royal ancestors. In like manner, Christ is called *a shoot that will spring from the stem of Jesse, and a branch from his roots (Isa 11:1; Jer 23:5; Zech 3:8; 6:12)*. It is interesting that the term, initially applied to the Messiah, is now applied to Christians, who are called *branches of Christ, the Vine*, because of their union with Him (John 15:5-6).

Now consider being a *new creation*.

• *A new Creation*

Paul is telling us about one of the more important doctrines in Christianity: a *new creation*.

But how do we become a *new creation*? The answer is clear: when we are *in Christ*, we will become a *new creation*. One act leads to the other; the terms are inseparable. If we are one, then we will become the other. We need to become both; we must be *in Christ*; we must be a *new creation*. We must be *in Christ* so that we will bear much fruit and do good works. When we are *in Christ,* we will be led by the Spirit and we will walk in the truth of the Spirit. When we are *in Christ*, we will know and experience the fullness of the Spirit of God.

The fruit of the Spirit (Gal 5:22) and good works are the evidence of being *in Christ*. Why are good works the evidence of being *in Christ* and being a *new creation*? Because we are God's workmanship and because we have been *created in Christ* and the purpose for which we have been created in Christ is to do good works.

For we are his workmanship, created in Christ Jesus for good works, which God prepared beforehand, that we should walk in them. (Eph 2:10 RSV)

To be a *new creation* is to have faith of which good works are the evidence of faith. Paul and James agree on the importance of faith, accompanied by good works. Faith and works are inseparable. This passage from James 2:14-25 summarizes the argument.

What does it profit, my brethren, if a man says he has faith but has not works? Can his faith save him? If a brother or sister is ill-clad and in lack of daily food, and one of you says to them, "Go in peace, be warmed and filled," without giving them the things needed for the body, what does it profit? So faith by itself, if it has no works, is dead. But someone will say, "You have faith and I have works." Show me your faith apart from your works, and I by my works will show you my faith. You believe that God is one; you do well. Even the demons believe - and shudder. Do you want to be shown, you shallow man, that faith apart from works is barren? Was not Abraham our father justified by works, when he offered his son Isaac upon the altar? You see that faith was active along with his works, and faith was completed by works, and the scripture was fulfilled which says, "Abraham believed God, and it was reckoned to him as righteousness"; and he was called the friend of God. You see that a man is justified by works and not by faith alone. (James 2:14-25 RSV)

We are called to be a *new creation* for at least three reasons: *first,* so that we would have the Mind of Christ (Phil 2:5); *second,* so that the ways and thoughts of God will be our ways and our thoughts (Isa 55:11); *third,* so that we, as a *new creation,* will share the glory of the New Heaven and the New Earth as part of God's new creation (Rev 21:1-4).

Christians have a unique responsibility in becoming a *new creation*: *first,* to be led/walk by the Spirit; *second,* to be *crucified* with Christ; *third,* to die to self and be alive in Christ; *fourth,* to respond in faith to the love of God; *fifth,* to accept and live in the freedom offered through Christ; *sixth,* to be obedient to the Law of Christ; *seventh,* to have Christ formed in us and Christ living in us.

When we can do all that, then we will now have the fullness of the *new creation,* we will be *in Christ.*

Christ came so that we would become a *new creation.*

if anyone is in Christ, he is a new creation (2 Cor 5:17 RSV)

We have now completed the eight (8) reasons for the Incarnation as related *To Serve God,* as well as the twelve (12) reasons which are related *To Bring Salvation.*

We now turn to the two (2) reasons for the Incarnation as related *To Fulfill the Scriptures.*

3. To Fulfill The Scriptures (2)

Chapter 26. I have not come to abolish them but to fulfill them (Matt 5:17 RSV)

Chapter 27. But this is to fulfill the scripture (John 13:18)

Because of Love, He came …

Chapter 26. I have come not to abolish them but to fulfill them. (Matt 5:17 RSV)

Think not that I have come to abolish the law and the prophets; **I have come not to abolish them but to fulfill them.** *(Matt 5:17 RSV)*

Yet the LORD warned Israel and Judah by every prophet and every seer, saying, "Turn from your evil ways and keep my commandments and my statutes, in accordance with all the law which I commanded your fathers, and which I sent to you by my servants the prophets." (2 Kings 17:13 RSV)

For the law was given through Moses; grace and truth came through Jesus Christ. (John 1:17 RSV)

God has set forth His laws, as the basis for both the spiritual and physical conduct of His people. In addition, when the situation warranted, He sent His prophets to warn the people of the evil in their lives and the judgment that would follow if not corrected.

Now, with the Incarnation, Jesus Christ came to bring a renewed understanding of the original intent of the Law and the Prophets.

The Scriptures emphasize that the Law and the Prophets are closely interconnected. The Law was given through Moses to define the standard for the conduct of the Israelites, as individuals and as a nation; the Prophets were sent by God when the conduct of the Israelites was opposed to the expressed will of God. Let us look at these in more detail.

I begin with the Law.

The Law is that combination of laws given by God to Moses which

145

begin with the Ten Commandments, as stated in Exodus 20:3-17 and Deuteronomy 5:7-21. However, many other biblical laws were given by God. Biblical law is more than a statement of human law. It is an expression of what God requires of man. It rests on the eternal moral principles that are consistent with the very nature of God Himself. Therefore, moral law is the summary of biblical law. As such it sets forth fundamental and universal moral principles. The civil law includes those specific laws in the Pentateuch that define and regulate civil and social behavior. All such laws are basically religious since God is the lawgiver and ruler over everything. The Jews had made a meticulous study of the Old Testament and found that there were 365 commandments (*you shall …*) and 248 prohibitions (*you shall not …*), making a total of 613 rules and regulations. This, they considered, was the Law of Moses; this was the biblical law.

In principal, the Law was given to reveal sin (Rom 5:13), which is rebellion and disobedience. Anything that is contrary to God's will and God's standard is sin.

Now, the foundation of that biblical law was both the love and the wrath of God. And the foundation of all of the law was the two great commandments: we are to love the Lord, our God, and we are to love our neighbor.

Such is briefly the *law*.

Now, consider the *prophets*.

The prophets were those who were called by God to communicate faithfully and courageously God's messages to the nation of Israel. Generally the prophets were sent by God when the nations of Israel and Judah were unfaithful in fulfilling His law. In that regard, the prophets were to proclaim the word of God as it related to specific events, actions, and conduct. The prophets rarely forecasted the future; their role was to express the judgment of God and to warn them of serious consequences from God if ungodly conditions continued. The prophets were *warners* from God of the consequence of continued sin.

Their primary role was to bear God's word for the purpose of teaching, reproving, correcting, and training in righteousness (2 Tim 3:16). They warned of impending danger for continued disobedience or they disclosed God's will to the people. Prophets were referred to as *messengers of the Lord* (Isa 44:26; Hag 1:13), *servants of God* (Amos 3:7), *shepherds* (Zech 11:4, 7; Jer 17:16), and *watchmen* (Isa 62:6).

Except for God's call and His direction, prophets had no special qualifications. They came from all walks of life and all classes of society. They included farmers like Amos (Amos 7:14) and Elisha (1 Kings 19:19), princes like Abraham (Gen 23:6), and priests like Ezekiel (Ezek 1:3). Women and children also were prophets (1 Sam 3:19-20; 2 Kings 22:14).

However, a prophet spoke with the authority of God through the power of the Holy Spirit (Num 11:29; 24:4). They shared one characteristic: a faithful proclamation of God's word and not their own (Jer 23:16; Ezek 13:2). Jesus' reference to Himself as a prophet (John 12:49-50) is because He faithfully repeated God's word to man.

There was a basic message from all of these prophets. *First,* God is holy, just, and loving. He cannot abide sin. *Second*, any individual or nation which continues to sin, unless repentant, will face serious consequences. *Third,* no individual or any nation is immune from the judgment of God. *Fourth*, it is extremely dangerous to ignore the warnings of God.

The Scriptures contain 16 Books which relate to the Prophets; four are considered Major Prophets (Isaiah, Jeremiah, Ezekiel, and Daniel) while 12 are considered Minor Prophets. That distinction has nothing to do with the importance of their prophetic calling; it only relates to the brevity of their writings, not with the significance of their message. For example, Isaiah has 66 chapters; Obadiah has only 19 verses.

Further, the 16 Books of the Prophets are divided into 4 groups:

1. The prophets of Israel (northern Kingdom): Hosea, Amos, Joel, Jonah.
2. The prophets of Judah (southern Kingdom): Isaiah, Jeremiah, Obadiah, Micah, Nahum, Habakkuk, Zephaniah.
3. The prophets of the Captivity: Ezekiel, Daniel.
4. The prophets of the Restoration: Haggai, Zechariah, Malachi.

Most of the prophets remain obscure which indicates that their message required face-to-face confrontation and a spoken rather than a written message. Many times the prophet stood alone and spoke to an unsympathetic or even antagonistic audience. Great courage and independence of spirit were required.

In addition to the 16 prophets mentioned, there are thousands of prophets unnamed in the Bible; consider just two examples of this truth:

After that you shall come to Gibeath-elohim, where there is a garrison of the Philistines; and there, as you come to the city, you will meet a band of prophets coming down from the high place with harp, tambourine, flute, and lyre before them, prophesying. Then the spirit of the LORD will come mightily upon you, and you shall prophesy with them and be turned into another man. Now when these signs meet you, do whatever your hand finds to do, for God is with you. (1 Sam 10:5-7 RSV)

And Jehoshaphat said to the king of Israel, "Inquire first for the word of the LORD." Then the king of Israel gathered the prophets together, about four hundred men, and said to them, "Shall I go to battle against Ramoth Gilead, or shall I forbear?" And they said, "Go up; for the Lord will give it into the hand of the king. (1 Kings 22:5-6 RSV)

In addition, some prophetic messages are extensive; others are extremely brief. For example, Jonah spoke 8 words to the great city of Nineveh (about 170,000 people), and the Assyrian Empire was converted. *Yet 40 days and Nineveh shall be overthrown.* Remarkable evangelism!

However, the prophets were persecuted and suffered greatly for their obedience to God, but they remained true to the witness to which God had called them.

I [God] have spoken to you persistently, but you have not listened to me. I have sent to you all my servants the prophets, sending them persistently, saying, 'Turn now every one of you from his evil way, and amend your doings, and do not go after other gods to serve them, and then you shall dwell in the land which I gave to you and your fathers.' But you did not incline your ear or listen to me. (Jer 35:14-16 RSV)

For example, in the New Testament, Jesus blessed the prophets who would receive a heavenly reward.

Blessed are you when men revile you and persecute you and utter all kinds of evil against you falsely on my account. Rejoice and be glad, for your reward is great in heaven, for so men persecuted the prophets who were before you. (Matt 5:11-12 RSV)

So, why did God send His prophets?

For several reasons: the people had forgotten who God was/is, what He had done, and the holiness to which He had called them. They forgot that God told them: *You shall be a people holy to the Lord. (Deut 7:6)*. Here the sense of holiness is that the people would be *set apart* for the things of God and *be different* in the manner in which they lived. They would not be like other nations; they would not do what they did.

They despised his [God's] statutes, and his covenant that he made with their fathers, and the warnings which he gave them. They went after false idols, and became false, and they followed the nations that were round about them, concerning whom the LORD had commanded them that they should not do like them. (2 Kings 17:15 RSV)

They did things that God had forbidden. Their sins included every form of evil: spiritual adultery, corruption, apostasy, idolatry, without social conscience, ignoring the prospect of divine judgment, violating God's laws, and distorting justice. They were proud, arrogant, immoral, unjust, disobedient, stiff-necked, rebellious, and unrighteous.

They thought that they were immune from the judgment of God. They thought that they were the chosen people of God who would receive only love and not wrath.

Many times, God reached out to the Israelites: specifically, He turned to the nation four times in the Book of Amos. God said, in spite of your evil and my warnings: *and yet you did not return to me. (Amos 4:6, 8, 9, 10)*

And consider the consequences: Israel, the northern kingdom, fell to the Assyrians in 722 BC. Judah, the southern kingdom, fell to the Babylonians in 586 BC. These kingdoms would never rise again.

The Law and the Prophets are holy to God.

Therefore, Jesus said: *Do not think that I have come to abolish the Law or the Prophets; I have not come to abolish them but to fulfill them. (Matt 5:17-18)*

Jesus showed great respect for the Law because it divinely represented the will of God for His people.

Jesus showed great respect for the Prophets because they were the divine messengers of God.

So how did Jesus Christ fulfill the law?

He did so by giving a new and fuller dimension to the two great commandments, which are to love God (Deut 6:5) and to love our neighbor (Lev 19:18).

Here is what He said: *A new command I [Christ] give you: Love one another. As I have loved you, so you must love one another. By this all men will know that you are my disciples, if you love one another. (John 13:34-35 RSV)*

Christ gave fullness to the Law and the Prophets that had not been present before.

It was this: the love of Christ is the measure by which everyone is to fulfill the Law and the Prophets.

Before there was no measurement: now Christ's love is the measurement.

When we understand His love and when we apply love to the Law and the Prophets, then we will begin to understand more fully the Laws, God's divine instruction, and God's divine warnings.

I have come not to abolish them but to fulfill them. (Matt 5:18 RSV)

Because of Love, He came …

Chapter 27. But this is to fulfill the scripture (John 13:18)

The Spirit of the Sovereign LORD is on me, because the LORD has anointed me to preach good news to the poor. He has sent me to bind up the brokenhearted, to proclaim freedom for the captives and release from darkness for the prisoners, to proclaim the year of the LORD's favor and the day of vengeance of our God, to comfort all who mourn, and provide for those who grieve in Zion — to bestow on them a crown of beauty instead of ashes, the oil of gladness instead of mourning, and a garment of praise instead of a spirit of despair. They will be called oaks of righteousness, a planting of the LORD for the display of his splendor. (Isa 61:1-3)

I am not referring to all of you; I know those I have chosen. **But this is to fulfill the scripture***: 'He who shares my bread has lifted up his heel against me.' (John 13:18)*

Every day I was with you, teaching in the temple courts, and you did not arrest me. But the Scriptures must be fulfilled. (Mark 14:49)

Our subject, relating to the Incarnation, is the *fulfillment* of the Scriptures.

Therefore, we begin with the understanding that *fulfillment* is the achievement or verification of something promised or predicted. So, regarding the Christ, what had been promised or predicted?

An examination of the Scriptures reveals 38 prophecies concerning Christ. In the discussion that follows, it is understood that *Messiah* is the Old Testament term which is translated *Christ* in the New Testament.

Christ has come to fulfill the Scriptures, primarily regarding Himself, as well as to bring glory to God.

Twelve (12) examples of the fulfillment of prophecies have been selected to verify the remaining 26.

- *Promised Offspring of Abraham: Gen 18:18; Acts 3:25; Matt 1:1; Luke 3:34*

Gen 18:18: Abraham will surely become a great and powerful nation, and all nations on earth will be blessed through him.

Acts 3:25: And you are heirs of the prophets and of the covenant God made with your fathers. He said to Abraham, 'Through your offspring all peoples on earth will be blessed.'

- *The Heir to the throne of David: Isa 9:7—Matt 1:1*

Isa 9:7: Of the increase of his government and peace there will be no end. He will reign on David's throne and over his kingdom, establishing and upholding it with justice and righteousness from that time on and forever. The zeal of the LORD Almighty will accomplish this.

Matt 1:1: A record of the genealogy of Jesus Christ the son of David, the son of Abraham:

- *Place of Birth: Mic 5:2—Matt 2:1, Luke 2:4-7*

Mic 5:2: But you, Bethlehem Ephrathah, though you are small among the clans of Judah, out of you will come for me one who will be ruler over Israel, whose origins are from of old, from ancient times.

Matt 2:1: After Jesus was born in Bethlehem in Judea, during the time of King Herod, Magi from the east came to Jerusalem.

- *As a Prophet: Deut 18:15—John 6:14*

Deut 18:15: The LORD your God will raise up for you a prophet like me from among your own brothers. You must listen to him.

John 6:14: After the people saw the miraculous sign that Jesus did, they began to say, "Surely this is the Prophet who is to come into the world."

- *As a Priest, like Melchizedek: Psa 110:4—Heb 6:20*

Psa 110:4: The LORD has sworn and will not change his mind: "You are a priest forever, in the order of Melchizedek."

Heb 6:20: … where Jesus, who went before us, has entered on our behalf. He has become a high priest forever, in the order of Melchizedek.

- *His rejection by the Jews: Isa 53:3—John 1:11*

Isa 53:3: He was despised and rejected by men, a man of sorrows, and familiar with suffering. Like one from whom men hide their faces he was despised, and we esteemed him not.

John 1:11: He came to that which was his own, but his own did not receive him.

- *His triumphal entry: Zech 9:9—John 12:13-14*

Zech 9:9: Rejoice greatly, O Daughter of Zion! Shout, Daughter of Jerusalem! See, your king comes to you, righteous and having salvation, gentle and riding on a donkey, on a colt, the foal of a donkey.

John 12:13-15: They took palm branches and went out to meet him, shouting, "Hosanna!" "Blessed is he who comes in the name of the Lord!" "Blessed is the King of Israel!" Jesus found a young donkey and sat upon it, as it is written, "Do not be afraid, O Daughter of Zion; see, your king is coming, seated on a donkey's colt."

- *Hated without cause: Psa 69:4—John 15:23-25*

Psa 69:4: Those who hate me without reason outnumber the hairs of my head; many are my enemies without cause, those who seek to destroy me. I am forced to restore what I did not steal.

John 15:23-25: He who hates me hates my Father as well. If I had not done among them what no one else did, they would not be guilty of sin. But now they have seen these miracles, and yet they have hated both me and my Father. But this is to fulfill what is written in their Law: 'They hated me without reason.'

- *Crucified with sinners: Isa 53:12—Matt 27:38*

Isa 53:12 Therefore I will give him a portion among the great, and he will divide the spoils with the strong, because he poured out his life unto death, and was numbered with the transgressors. For he bore the sin of many, and made intercession for the transgressors.

Matt 27:38: Two robbers were crucified with him, one on his right and one on his left.

- *Mocked and insulted: Psa 22:6-8—Matt 27:39-40*

Psa 22:6-8: But I am a worm and not a man, scorned by men and despised by the people. All who see me mock me; they hurl insults, shaking their heads: "He trusts in the LORD; let the LORD rescue him. Let him deliver him, since he delights in him."

Matt 27:39-40: Those who passed by hurled insults at him, shaking their heads and saying, "You who are going to destroy the temple and build it in three days, save yourself! Come down from the cross, if you are the Son of God!"

- *His resurrection: Psa 16:10—Matt 28:9*

Ps 16:10: … because you will not abandon me to the grave, nor will you let your Holy One see decay.

Matt 28:9: Suddenly Jesus met them. "Greetings," he said. They came to him, clasped his feet and worshiped him.

- *His ascension: Psa 68:18—Luke 24:50-51; Acts 1:9*

Ps 68:18: When you ascended on high, you led captives in your train; you received gifts from men, even from the rebellious — that you, O LORD God, might dwell there.

Luke 24:50-51: When he had led them out to the vicinity of Bethany, he lifted up his hands and blessed them. While he was blessing them, he left them and was taken up into heaven.

All of the Old Testament prophecies regarding Christ have been fulfilled in the New Testament. This is the witness of God's Word.

Jesus Christ had come to fulfill what had been promised.

But this is to fulfill the scriptures (John 13:18)

This completes the reasons for the Incarnation as regarding: *To Fulfill the Scriptures.*

We now turn to the fourth category, *To Transform The World*

4. To Transform The World (8)

Chapter 28. I have come into the world as a light (John 12:46 RSV)

Chapter 29. for this I came into the world, to testify to the truth (John 18:37)

Chapter 30. on this rock I will build my church (Matt 16:18)

Chapter 31. Go therefore and make disciples of all nations (Matt 28:19 RSV)

Chapter 32. I have come to bring fire on the earth (Lk 12:49)

Chapter 33. For judgment I have come into this world (John 9:39)

Chapter 34. The reason the Son of God appeared was to destroy the devil's work (1 John 3:8)

Chapter 35. See, I have told you ahead of time (Matt 24:25)

Because of Love, He came …

Chapter 28. I have come as light into the world (John 12:46 RSV)

Again Jesus spoke to them, saying, "I am the light of the world; he who follows me will not walk in darkness, but will have the light of life. (John 8:12 RSV)

*And Jesus cried out and said, "He who believes in me [Christ], believes not in me but in him who sent me. And he who sees me sees him who sent me. **I have come as light into the world**, that whoever believes in me may not remain in darkness. (John 12:44-46 RSV)*

Another reason for the Incarnation was that Christ had come as light into the world so that the lost would not remain in darkness. Jesus Christ now defines an additional symbol that will identify Him in the world: *I have come as light.*

In the various symbols representing His Person, Jesus had also come as the Bread of Life (John 6:35), as the Good Shepherd (John 10:11), as the resurrection and the life (11:25), as the Way, the Truth, and the Life (John 14:6), and as the Vine and we as the branches (John 15:5).

Now Christ comes into the world as a Light.

So how do we understand so powerful and yet so familiar a simile? An examination of the Scriptures will provide insight to understand what Christ is saying.

Christ said: *I am the light of the world.* When you see Me, you see the *Light.*

So let's follow where the Scriptures take us.

In the Scriptures, light symbolizes God's presence, His truth, His holiness, His purity, and His righteous and redemptive activities. The Scriptures also refer to God as the *light* to guide His people.

God is light (1 John 1:5 RSV); when we walk in the light, we shall be purified from all sin.

This is the message we have heard from him and proclaim to you, that God is light and in him is no darkness at all. If we say we have fellowship with him while we walk in darkness, we lie and do not live according to the truth; but if we walk in the light, as he is in the light, we have fellowship with one another, and the blood of Jesus his Son cleanses us from all sin. (1 John 1:5-7 RSV)

The Psalms declare: *The Lord is my light and my salvation; whom shall I fear? (Ps 27:1 RSV)*

God's Word, the Bible, is a lamp for the believer. *Your word is a lamp to my feet and a light to my path (Psa 119:105).*

Since Jesus Christ is the fullness of the deity (Col 2:9 RSV), that which is in God the Father must also be in God the Son.

The Father and the Son are One: if God is light, then Christ must also be light.

Therefore, the Scriptures identify Jesus Christ as divine illumination: *I am the light of the world (John 8:12 RSV)*. Because He is the light of the world, those who accept this light will inherit eternal life; those who reject this divine light would bring *judgment* upon themselves (John 3:19-21 RSV).

Again Jesus spoke to them, saying, "I am the light of the world; he who follows me will not walk in darkness, but will have the light of life." (John 8:12 RSV)

This theme of light is a message in the Scriptures from the beginning to the end.

I begin with the beginning: *And God said, "Let there be light"; and there was light. And God saw that the light was good; and God separated the light from the darkness. God called the light Day, and the darkness he called Night. And there was evening and there was morning, one day. (Gen 1:3-5 RSV)*

In addition, I end with the ending: *There shall no more be anything accursed, but the throne of God and of the Lamb shall be in it, and his servants shall worship him; they shall see his face, and his name shall be on their foreheads. And night shall be no more; they need no light of lamp or sun, for the Lord God will be their light, and they shall reign forever and ever. (Rev 22:3-5 RSV)*

In between Genesis and Revelation, there is this message of the divine significance of light, that God created the light, that God sent light in the Person of His Son, and that, at the end of the Age, the Lord God will be the light.

These thoughts are all centered on this declaration from Jesus Christ: *I come as Light.*

So let us examine eight passages which address this subject of Christ as Light.

First, John 12:44-46 RSV: Then Jesus cried out, "When a man believes in me [Christ], he does not believe in me only, but in the one who sent me. When he looks at me, he sees the one who sent me. I have come into the world as a light, so that no one who believes in me should stay in darkness."

There are several valuable theological messages here. *First,* there is the message of *believing in Christ.* Recall the passage regarding Abraham, God and righteousness. *Abraham believed God and it was credited to him as righteousness.* (Rom 4:3 RSV; James 2:23 RSV). In like manner, believing in Christ leads to righteousness; the more we believe in God the Son, the greater becomes our righteousness. Our righteousness is the measure of our trust and faith in God. Christ also stated that belief in Him also involves belief in God, the Father, the One who sent Him. If we believe in Christ, the companion to that is belief in God. To accept One is to accept the Other. Christ claimed that He and the Father are One. When you see Christ, you see the Father. As Paul stated in *Colossians 1:15-16 RSV: He is the image of the invisible God, the first-born of all creation; for in him all things were created, in heaven and on earth, visible and invisible, whether thrones or dominions or principalities or authorities - all things were created through him and for him.*

Further, Christ claims that He is Light: therefore, those who believe in Him, who trust Him, will never remain in darkness. The Light of the world has come to disperse the darkness of the world.

Second, Matthew 17:2 RSV: And he was transfigured before them, and his face shone like the sun, and his garments became white as light.

We now come face to face with the doctrine of the Transfiguration.

The transfiguration is simply this: what was on the inside of the Son of God was now visible on the outside. On this occasion, God gave Christ honor and glory for His disciples to see (2 Peter 1:17) and for them to witness to the world. This Person, this Jesus of Nazareth, had truly been sent by God and was duly honored by God. It is interesting that, at this occasion, both Moses and Elijah also appeared. It is interesting also that a cloud overshadowed Jesus during His Transfiguration. This cloud at the Transfiguration is symbolic of the event during the Exodus when God appeared to Moses on Mt. Sinai (Ex 24) and when God also spoke from a cloud (Ex 40:34-38).

He [Peter] was still speaking, when lo, a bright cloud overshadowed them, and a voice from the cloud said, "This is my beloved Son, with whom I am well pleased; listen to him." (Matt 17:5 RSV)

When the disciples heard that Jesus was God's beloved Son, the chosen one with whom He was well pleased, they probably remembered Psalm 2:7; Isaiah 42:1, and Genesis 22:2. Above all, they must have remembered God's *voice* at Jesus' baptism.

And when Jesus was baptized, he went up immediately from the water, and behold, the heavens were opened and he saw the Spirit of God descending like a dove, and alighting on him; and lo, a voice from heaven, saying, "This is my beloved Son, with whom I am well pleased." (Matt 3:16-17 RSV)

In many regards, the words and actions at the Transfiguration closely resemble those at the baptism of Christ. In fact, the recorded words of God at the Transfiguration are identical to the words which God spoke at Christ's baptism (Matt 3:16-17 RSV).

Further, two other statements are made regarding Christ's appearance: first, His face shown like the sun; second, His clothes became as white as the light. This dazzling scene was beyond comprehension. Can anyone possibly imagine someone's face shining like the sun? Can anyone imagine clothes as white as light? I believe that the event was so overwhelming that the witnesses could not think of any other way to describe His appearance. I believe that these statements express the supernatural event that took place.

Third: Luke 2:29-32 RSV: Lord, now let thou thy servant depart in peace, according to thy word; for mine eyes have seen thy salvation which thou hast prepared in the presence of all peoples, a light for revelation to the Gentiles, and for glory to thy people Israel. (Luke 2:29-32 RSV)

We now turn to the Nunc Dimittis, which is the prayer of Simeon, as he held the baby Jesus and realized that he was looking into the Lord's Christ. Simeon is described as follows: *Now there was a man in Jerusalem, whose name was Simeon, and this man was righteous and devout, looking for the consolation of Israel, and the Holy Spirit was upon him. And it had been revealed to him by the Holy Spirit that he should not see death before he had seen the Lord's Christ. And inspired by the Spirit he came into the temple; and when the parents brought in the child Jesus, to do for him according to the custom of the law, (Luke 2:25-27 RSV).* Simeon took the baby, Jesus, into his arms: he knew that he had seen the salvation of God in the face of Christ. This salvation is for all people, because the Christ would be a *light for revelation to the Gentiles and for glory to your people Israel.*

Fourth: John 1:4-9 RSV: In him was life, and the life was the light of men. The light shines in the darkness, and the darkness has not overcome it. There was a man sent from God, whose name was John. He came for testimony, to bear witness to the light, that all might believe through him. He was not the light, but came to bear witness to the light. The true light that enlightens every man was coming into the world. (John 1:4-9 RSV)

Consider the monumental truths in this passage. In Christ alone is salvation and that salvation brings people out of the darkness of this world into the Light which is Jesus Christ. *Salvation is found in no one else, for there is no other name under heaven given to men by which we must be saved. (Acts 4:12 RSV)*

Christ, the Light, penetrated the darkness, which was representative of sin in the world, and the evil world cannot understand the Presence and glory of Christ. As a witness to His Christ, God sent John the Baptist to testify concerning Christ with the express purpose that all men might believe; and, through their faith, they would recognize, acknowledge, and receive the true light, Christ, which is offered to all.

Fifth: John 3:19-21 RSV: And this is the judgment, that the light has come into the world, and men loved darkness rather than light, because their deeds were evil. For every one who does evil hates the light, and does not come to the light, lest his deeds should be exposed. But he who does what is true comes to the light, that it may be clearly seen that his deeds have been wrought in God. (John 3:19-21 RSV)

Here again, the apostle John emphasized the difference between light and darkness, the difference between righteousness and sin, the difference between obedience and rebellion. This theme is played over and over again in the Scriptures. Light exposes the darkness which represents the evil deeds of evil men. If men are evil, they choose to remain in the darkness. If men seek righteousness and live by the truth, they will seek Christ, the Light of the world, and seek the ways of God, revealed through His Son, Jesus Christ.

Sixth: John 12:35-36 RSV: Jesus said to them, "The light is with you for a little longer. Walk while you have the light, lest the darkness overtake you; he who walks in the darkness does not know where he goes. While you have the light, believe in the light, that you may become sons of light." (John 12:35-36 RSV)

Jesus told His disciples that He would be with them just a little while longer. In the time available, Christ taught them to learn to *walk* in the light, to learn what it means to be righteous, to grow in faith so that nothing will detract them from the life within the Light. If our trust is in Christ, we will become the children of God and children of the Light. Since God is Light, His children are the children of the Light.

Seventh: I John 1:5-7 RSV: This is the message we have heard from him [Christ] and proclaim to you, that God is light and in him is no darkness at all. If we say we have fellowship with him while we walk in darkness, we lie and do not live according to the truth; but if we walk in the light, as he is in the light, we have fellowship with one another, and the blood of Jesus his Son cleanses us from all sin. (1 John 1:5-7 RSV)

The apostle John makes this great affirmation: *God is light; in him there is no darkness at all.* This is a two-fold affirmation. Not only is God light, but it is a purity in which there is no darkness at all. There is no evidence of any evil in the holy and righteous God. If we have fellowship with God, then there can be no evidence of any sin in our lives. We must be pure and righteous as He is pure and righteous. We must be light, with no evidence and presence of any darkness. The result of this purity is that we have fellowship with like-minded believers—and the ultimate result is that the blood of Christ has purified us from all sin. We are forgiven and declared innocent of all sin; we are pardoned and have been set free.

Eighth: Ephesians 5:8-14 RSV: For once you were darkness, but now you are light in the Lord; walk as children of light (for the fruit of light is found in all that is good and right and true), and try to learn what is pleasing to the Lord. Take no part in the unfruitful works of darkness, but instead expose them. For it is a shame even to speak of the things that they do in secret; but when anything is exposed by the light it becomes visible, for anything that becomes visible is light. Therefore it is said, "Awake, O sleeper, and arise from the dead, and Christ shall give you light."

Here again, the apostle Paul turned to the relationship between darkness and light. He is totally consistent with the apostle John. Now Paul addressed those who had previously been in darkness (life of sin) and now are in the Light of the Son of God. Further, Paul stressed that light consists of goodness, righteousness, and truth. If we are in the light, those will be the attributes and reflections of our lives. People who see us will see Christ: those people will also see love, faith, joy, peace, righteousness and truth in our lives and in our actions. We are to wake up so that Christ will shine on us which means that we are the approved of God because of what we have received, what we have believed and what we have done as a witness to the Light of the world.

I [Christ] have come as light into the world (John 12:46 RSV)
Because of Love, He came …

Chapter 29. for this I came into the world, to testify to the truth (John 18:37)

Pilate then went back inside the palace, summoned Jesus and asked him, "Are you the king of the Jews?" "Is that your own idea," Jesus asked, "or did others talk to you about me?" "Am I a Jew?" Pilate replied. "It was your people and your chief priests who handed you over to me. What is it you have done?" Jesus said, "My kingdom is not of this world. If it were, my servants would fight to prevent my arrest by the Jews. But now my kingdom is from another place."

*"You are a king, then!" said Pilate. Jesus answered, "You are right in saying I am a king. In fact, for this reason I was born, and **for this I came into the world, to testify to the truth**. Everyone on the side of truth listens to me." "What is truth?" Pilate asked. With this he went out again to the Jews and said, "I find no basis for a charge against him. But it is your custom for me to release to you one prisoner at the time of the Passover. Do you want me to release 'the king of the Jews'?" They shouted back, "No, not him! Give us Barabbas!" Now Barabbas had taken part in a rebellion. (John 18:33-40)*

We have, in this passage from John, this great exchange between Jesus Christ and Pontius Pilate, just prior to the crucifixion.

In a way, this is the trial of Jesus before the Roman authorities on the charge of sedition against the Roman Empire for claiming to be a king. However, in this exchange, the Jewish authorities became judge and jury: they are the ones who demand of the Romans the crucifixion of the innocent Son of God.

In this exchange, Jesus states another reason for the Incarnation which is to testify to the truth.

In this courtroom scene, Christ took the stand to testify to one of the important reasons that He had come into the world. He came to testify to the truth. The truth is on trial: Jesus Christ is the Witness to the truth.

Truth: no term is more familiar and yet is more difficult to define than *truth*.

It is like the word, *love*, equally familiar and equally difficult to define.

God is truth; the Spirit is truth; and Jesus is truth. Jesus said, "*I am the way, the truth, and the life. No one comes to the Father except through Me.*" *(John 14:6)*

Jesus and the revelation which the Spirit of truth gave through His apostles are the ultimate definition of truth about God, man, redemption, history, and the world. *The law was given through Moses, but grace and truth came through Jesus Christ. (John 1:17)*

So what is the *truth* which describes Christ and for which He came into the world?

Let's explore the Scriptures which speak at great length about this word, *truth*.

Into your hands I commit my spirit; redeem me, O LORD, the God of truth. (Ps 31:5)

Send forth your light and your truth, let them guide me; let them bring me to your holy mountain, to the place where you dwell. (Ps 43:3)

He will judge the world in righteousness and the peoples in his truth. (Ps 96:13)

I have not spoken in secret, from somewhere in a land of darkness; I have not said to Jacob's descendants, 'Seek me in vain.' I, the LORD, speak the truth; I declare what is right. (Isa 45:19)

but first I will tell you what is written in the Book of Truth … (Dan 10:21)

This is what the LORD says: "I will return to Zion and dwell in Jerusalem. Then Jerusalem will be called the City of Truth, and the mountain of the LORD Almighty will be called the Holy Mountain." (Zech 8:3)

But when he, the Spirit of truth, comes, he will guide you into all truth. (John 16:13)

Sanctify them by the truth; your word is truth. (John 17:17)

The wrath of God is being revealed from heaven against all the godlessness and wickedness of men who suppress the truth by their wickedness, since what may be known about God is plain to them, because God has made it plain to them. (Rom 1:18-19)

Stand firm then, with the belt of truth buckled around your waist. (Eph 6:14)

the faith and love that spring from the hope that is stored up for you in heaven and that you have already heard about in the word of truth, the gospel that has come to you. (Col 1:5-6)

Do your best to present yourself to God as one approved, a workman who does not need to be ashamed and who correctly handles the word of truth. (2 Tim 2:15)

Let us summarize what these passages tell us about truth.

In both the Old and New Testaments, truth is the moral and personal quality of God. God proclaimed that He is *merciful and gracious, longsuffering, and abounding in goodness and truth (Ex 34:6)*. He is a *God of truth … without injustice (Deut 32:4)*. All of God's works, precepts, and judgments are done in righteousness and truth (Ps 96:13; 111:8). He is *the God of truth* (Isa 65:16). The psalmist declared, *Your law is truth* (119:142), *all Your commandments are truth* (119:151), and *the entirety of Your word is truth* (119:160). Because of His perfect nature and will, God has to speak and act in truth; He cannot lie (1 Sam 15:29; Heb 6:18; James 1:17-18).

Jesus is the Word of God who became flesh, *the only begotten of the Father, full of grace and truth (John 1:14)*. All Jesus said was true, because He told the truth which He heard from God (John 8:40). He promised His disciples that He would send *the Spirit of truth (John 14:17; 15:26; 16:13)* who would abide in us forever (John 14:16), who would testify about Jesus (John 15:26), and who would guide Christians into all truth (John 16:13), and glorify Jesus (John 16:14).

Seventy eight (78) times in the New Testament, Jesus said: *I tell you the truth …*

So what is *truth,* and what is the *truth* for which Christ came into the world to testify?

In the Scriptures, the word, *truth,* might well be understood as the Person of God and the revealed will of God.

Truth is related to God, to His Son, to the Spirit, and to God's word.

Truth is the revelation of God. Truth is contained in the Word of God.

Christ said: I have come to testify to the truth. Here is what I believe He is stating: I [Christ] have come to testify to God; I have come to testify to the things of God which must be accepted by all nations.

Truth is that God must be honored forever.

Truth is the revealed written Word of God.

Truth is the revealed living Word of God, His Son.

for this I came into the world, to testify to the truth (John 18:37)

Because of Love, He came ...

Chapter 30. on this rock I will build my church (Matt 16:18)

When Jesus came to the region of Caesarea Philippi, he asked his disciples, "Who do people say the Son of Man is?" They replied, "Some say John the Baptist; others say Elijah; and still others, Jeremiah or one of the prophets." "But what about you?" he asked. "Who do you say I am?" Simon Peter answered, "You are the Christ, the Son of the living God."

Jesus replied, "Blessed are you, Simon son of Jonah, for this was not revealed to you by man, but by my Father in heaven. And I tell you that you are Peter, and **on this rock I [Christ] will build my church,** *and the gates of Hades will not overcome it. I will give you the keys of the kingdom of heaven; whatever you bind on earth will be bound in heaven, and whatever you loose on earth will be loosed in heaven." Then he warned his disciples not to tell anyone that he was the Christ. (Matt 16:13-20)*

And he [Christ] is the head of the body, the church. (Col 1:18)

Another reason for the Incarnation was to establish the church of Jesus Christ, as an extension of the assembly of God which has been present ever since the time of Abraham. God has always had an *ekklesia*, an assembly of faithful believers, which began with Abraham and has been present ever since. The first mention of such a sacred assembly is in Exodus 12:16-18, when God commanded the Israelites to meet and celebrate the Feast of Unleavened Bread, as a lasting ordinance for generations to come.

However, there were times when the sins of the people led to God's wrath and judgment; in addition, there were times when devastating events scattered the people. In such events, God made provision for a faithful remnant to form the nucleus of a new community of faith, which was to be the church of Jesus Christ.

The LORD will scatter you among the peoples, and only a few of you will survive among the nations to which the LORD will drive you. There you will worship man-made gods of wood and stone, which cannot see or hear or eat or smell. But if from there you seek the LORD your God, you will find him if you look for him with all your heart and with all your soul. When you are in distress and all these things have happened to you, then in later days you will return to the LORD your God and obey him. For the LORD your God is a merciful God; he will not abandon or destroy you or forget the covenant with your forefathers, which he confirmed to them by oath. (Deut 4:27-31)

In that day the remnant of Israel, the survivors of the house of Jacob, will no longer rely on him who struck them down but will truly rely on the LORD, the Holy One of Israel. A remnant will return, a remnant of Jacob will return to the Mighty God. Though your people, O Israel, be like the sand by the sea, only a remnant will return. Destruction has been decreed, overwhelming and righteous. The Lord, the LORD Almighty, will carry out the destruction decreed upon the whole land. (Isa 10:20-23)

The Old Testament remnant of God is the foundation of the Christian church.

It is on this remnant of God that Christ came to establish His church.

The remnant of the *ekklesia* is also present in the New Testament when the apostle Paul applied the teaching of Isaiah and other prophets about the remnant for the church of Jesus Christ (Rom 11:5). Paul showed that God's purpose is seen in the *remnant* out of Israel who joined with the Gentiles to form the church, the new people of God. Further, Jesus' choice of twelve apostles is built upon remnant themes. Symbolizing the twelve tribes, the apostles became the *remnant* who erected a new spiritual structure, the church, whose foundation is Israel. In the church, both Jews and Gentiles, circumcised and uncircumcised, found their united spiritual home based upon faith alone in Christ alone.

The Apostle Paul understood the character of both the local church and the church universal. He wrote regarding its role and its responsibility in the following passages from The Epistle to the Ephesians.

In Ephesians 1:19-23, Paul emphasized the truth that God has appointed Christ *head over everything for the church, which is his body.*

In Ephesians 2:14-18, Paul stated that the *new man* will be the foundation of the *new church.* Christ will unite all nations under one Head. *For he himself [Christ] is our peace, who has made the two one and has destroyed the barrier, the dividing wall of hostility, by abolishing in his flesh the law with its commandments and regulations. His purpose was to create in himself one new man out of the two, thus making peace, and in this one body to reconcile both of them to God through the cross, by which he put to death their hostility. He came and preached peace to you who were far away and peace to those who were near. For through him we both have access to the Father by one Spirit. (Eph 2:14-18)*

In Ephesians 3:10-13, Paul stated that, *through the church, the manifold wisdom of God should be made known.* In addition, *through faith in him [Christ] we may approach God with freedom and confidence.*

His [God] intent was that now, through the church, the manifold wisdom of God should be made known to the rulers and authorities in the heavenly realms, according to his eternal purpose which he accomplished in Christ Jesus our Lord. In him and through faith in him we may approach God with freedom and confidence. I ask you, therefore, not to be discouraged because of my sufferings for you, which are your glory. (Eph 3:10-13)

In this church, Christ, who is the image of the invisible God, is also the Head of the body, which is the church.

He is the image of the invisible God, the firstborn over all creation. For by him all things were created: things in heaven and on earth, visible and invisible, whether thrones or powers or rulers or authorities; all things were created by him and for him. He is before all things, and in him all things hold together. And he is the head of the body, the church; he is the beginning and the firstborn from among the dead, so that in everything he might have the supremacy. For God was pleased to have all his fullness dwell in him, and through him to reconcile to himself all things, whether things on earth or things in heaven, by making peace through his blood, shed on the cross. (Col 1:15-20)

Regarding the church that Jesus Christ came to establish, two statements require clarification. The first relates to the question from Christ: *Who do you say I am?* To that question, Simon Peter answered: *You are the Christ, the Son of the living God.* Then Matthew reports this response from Jesus Christ: *And I tell you that you are Peter, and on this rock I will build my church.*

This later statement has been the source of unnecessary and unfortunate controversy in the Christian Church. The reason: the Protestant churches and the Roman Catholic Church have taken opposing theological views on the interpretation and application of this passage.

The Roman Catholic Church has maintained throughout history that the *rock* on which the church of Christ is to be built is the *person of Simon Peter*. After all, they say: isn't that what Christ said? That is why the Basilica in Rome is called the Basilica of Peter and Paul, so as to establish their position that the Roman Catholic Church has full and complete authority over all of Christianity—an authority given to Peter by Christ. They claim Peter as the first *Pope* and all others to be his direct successor, in an unbroken chain.

However, the Protestant church proclaims two theological positions which differ with the Roman Catholic claim. First, they maintain that the rock on which the Christian church is founded is not the person of Peter, but the confession that *Jesus is the Christ.* Second, they maintain that the apostles had no authority to confer apostleship on others.

Let us address these two issues, beginning with the statement: *on this rock, I will build my church.*

The Protestants deny that Christ said that He would build His church on the person of Peter. Instead, they say that the general sense of the *rock* as given throughout the Scriptures is clear and unmistakable.

So, what is the proper understanding of the *rock* on which Christ will build His church?

The Protestant church has maintained, through the years, that the *rock* which is referred to here is not the person of Peter, but rather the *confession of Peter: You are the Christ, the Son of the living God.*

Christ is the Rock on which the Christian church is built. Christ is the Head of the body, the church (Col 1:18). The truth of Scripture is the basis for this truth.

Throughout Scripture, God is constantly referred to as the *Rock*. As the Son of God, this designation equally applies to Him. There are 37 references in the Scriptures in which God or Christ are referred to as the *Rock*. Let me share a few.

But his bow remained steady, his strong arms stayed limber, because of the hand of the Mighty One of Jacob, because of the Shepherd, the Rock of Israel. (Gen 49:24)

He is the Rock, his works are perfect, and all his ways are just. A faithful God who does no wrong, upright and just is he. (Deut 32:4)

He abandoned the God who made him and rejected the Rock his Savior. (Deut 32:15)

The LORD is my rock, my fortress and my deliverer; my God is my rock, in whom I take refuge, my shield and the horn of my salvation. (2 Sam 22:2-3)

"The LORD lives! Praise be to my Rock! Exalted be God, the Rock, my Savior! (2 Sam 22:47)

The LORD is my rock, my fortress and my deliverer; my God is my rock, in whom I take refuge. (Ps 18:2)

The LORD lives! Praise be to my Rock! Exalted be God my Savior! (Ps 18:46)

They remembered that God was their Rock, that God Most High was their Redeemer. (Ps 78:35)

Come, let us sing for joy to the LORD; let us shout aloud to the Rock of our salvation. Let us come before him with thanksgiving. (Ps 95:1-2)

Trust in the LORD forever, for the LORD, the LORD, is the Rock eternal. (Isa 26:4)

They all ate the same spiritual food and drank the same spiritual drink; for they drank from the spiritual rock that accompanied them, and that rock was Christ. (1 Cor 10:3-4)

There is no evidence in the Scriptures in which any human being is referred to as a rock. Such a term, rock, is reserved for God and for Jesus Christ.

With particular reference to I Corinthians 10:3-4, it is clear that the rock was Christ. Christ is the Rock on which the Church of Christ is built.

Second, let us consider the authority of the apostles to convey apostleship on their successors.

When the apostles met to determine how to fill the void created by the unfaithfulness of Judas, it was determined that the person chosen *must become a witness with us of his resurrection. So they proposed two men: Joseph called Barsabbas (also known as Justus) and Matthias. (Acts 1:22-24)*

The key qualification was that the person must have been, like the other apostles, a witness to the resurrection of Christ.

Next, the eleven apostles prayed to Christ. *Lord, you know everyone's heart. Show us which of these two you have chosen to take over this apostolic ministry, (Acts 1:24-25)*

Look at the passage carefully. The apostles prayed: *which of the two you [Christ] have chosen.* They are not praying about anyone that they have chosen.

The choice of the replacement apostle was to be made by Jesus Christ.

I repeat: the apostles recognized that they had no authority to choose a replacement for Judas. Such authority resided only with Jesus Christ.

In addition, the apostles had no authority to determine their successors. Succession was never part of being an apostle. Christ made no provision and gave no authority for apostles to have or to select their successors.

Finally, the church, specific and universal, has a divine commission.

Then Jesus came to them [His disciples] and said, "All authority in heaven and on earth has been given to me. Therefore go and make disciples of all nations, baptizing them in the name of the Father and of the Son and of the Holy Spirit, and teaching them to obey everything I have commanded you. And surely I am with you always, to the very end of the age." (Matt 28:18-20)

The commission is clear; it is to do three things. First, *proclaim the gospel and witness to them* (make disciples of all nations); second, *baptize them* in the name of the Trinity; third, *teach them* to obey everything I [Christ] have commanded you.

Christ reinforced this commission just before His ascension, calling on His disciples to be His witnesses to the ends of the earth.

But you will receive power when the Holy Spirit comes on you; and you will be my witnesses in Jerusalem, and in all Judea and Samaria, and to the ends of the earth. (Acts 1:8)

Christ, who is the head of the body, is also the Son of God, who is God the Son.

Through His teachings and through His example, Jesus Christ has given us seven dimensions to the Christian church. It must be Christ-centered, Spirit-filled, Bible-believing, people of prayer, the salt of the earth, the light of the world, and witnesses to Christ, our Savior and Lord.

The church exists for those outside the church. The church exists to seek the lost, so that Christ would save them (Luke 19:10). The church points them to Christ.

And so, one important reason for the Incarnation was that Jesus Christ came *to establish His church.*

on this rock I will build my church (Matt 16:18)

Because of Love, He came ...

Chapter 31. Go therefore and make disciples of all nations (Matt 28:19 RSV)

And Jesus came and said to them, "All authority in heaven and on earth has been given to me. **Go therefore and make disciples of all nations,** *baptizing them in the name of the Father and of the Son and of the Holy Spirit, teaching them to observe all that I have commanded you; and lo, I am with you always, to the close of the age." (Matt 28:18-20 RSV)*

Salvation is found in no one else, for there is no other name under heaven given to men by which we must be saved. (Acts 4:12 RSV)

We now address another important reason for the Incarnation: it was so that Jesus Christ would teach His disciples to go and make disciples of all nations.

This is the commission that Christ gave His disciples; this is the commission for the church throughout the ages—and particularly so today.

Such a commission would not have been possible without the Incarnation. Christ came so that His church would be faithful in evangelism and that the gospel of Christ would be proclaimed to all nations.

And this gospel of the kingdom will be preached throughout the whole world, as a testimony to all nations; and then the end will come. (Matt 24:14 RSV)

Christ emphasized that the gospel must be preached to all nations before His Second Coming.

However, two questions immediately arise: first, what was the basis of Christ's authority? Second, what specifically were the commands of Christ?

By way of background, remember that God told Abraham that *all nations* would be blessed *(justified)* through you and your *offspring, who is Jesus Christ (Gen 22:18 RSV)*. That promise to Abraham was now to be fulfilled by both the Incarnation and this commission from Jesus Christ.

After His crucifixion and resurrection, Christ told His disciples to go into all the world and make disciples of *all nations*. The gospel is to be proclaimed to *all nations*.

The church is to spread the gospel of Christ and advance the Kingdom of God.

Consider the multiple themes in the three passages at the beginning of this chapter: the authority of Jesus Christ, evangelism, the universal nature of the gospel, obedience, baptism, teaching, the gospel, the Kingdom of God, the Holy Spirit, being a witness, the resurrection, and eternal life.

There is a great promise in these passages: *And surely I [Christ] am with you always, to the very end of the age. (Matt 28:20 RSV)* This promise is that Christ will be our companion in what He has commanded us to do. Now, certain passages from Paul are also included because I believe that what Paul taught reflected the truths that Paul had received from the Spirit and therefore are consistent with the teachings of Christ.

So, let us examine these reasons for the Incarnation.

The first question: what was the basis of Christ's authority? This is clear. His authority is from God, the Father. *When Jesus had spoken these words, he lifted up his eyes to heaven and said, "Father, the hour has come; glorify thy Son that the Son may glorify thee, since thou hast given him power over all flesh, to give eternal life to all whom thou hast given him. And this is eternal life, that they know thee the only true God, and Jesus Christ whom thou hast sent. (John 17:1-3 RSV)*

The second question: what did Christ command them to do? There are a multitude of topics of which I shall list only a few.

- To love one another: *A new commandment I [Christ] give to you, that you love one another; even as I have loved you, that you also love one another. By this all men will know that you are my disciples, if you have love for one another. (John 13:34-35 RSV)*

- The key truths in the Sermon on the Mount (Matt 5:1-7:27). In that passage, Christ identified in the Beatitudes those things of which God approved. Further, Christ taught of the need for a wider love, a deeper righteousness, and a nobler ambition. *But seek first his kingdom and his righteousness, and all these things shall be yours as well. (Matt 6:33 RSV)*

- The purpose of the cross: that through the Cross of Christ there would be forgiveness of sins to all who came to Christ as Savior and Lord. Further, at the cross, Christ took on our sins, and we received His righteousness. This spiritual exchange makes us the righteousness of God.

- The importance of forgiveness: *For if you forgive men their trespasses, your heavenly Father also will forgive you; but if you do not forgive men their trespasses, neither will your Father forgive your trespasses. (Matt 6:14-15 RSV)*

- The Fatherhood of God: Jesus taught of a new and personal God, who was to be addressed as *our Father,* and to whom we were to be His children. *But to all who received him, who believed in his name, he gave power to become children of God; who were born, not of blood nor of the will of the flesh nor of the will of man, but of God. (John 1:12-13 RSV)*

- The necessity of the new birth: *Jesus answered him, "Truly, truly, I say to you, unless one is born anew [again], he cannot see the kingdom of God." Nicodemus said to him, "How can a man be born when he is old? Can he enter a second time into his mother's womb and be born?" Jesus answered, "Truly, truly, I say to you, unless one is born of water and the Spirit, he cannot enter the kingdom of God. That which is born of the flesh is flesh, and that which is born of the Spirit is spirit. Do not marvel that I said to you, 'You must be born anew [again]. (John 3:3-7 RSV)*

- Do not be concerned about the things of this world: *If then you have been raised with Christ, seek the things that are above, where Christ is, seated at the right hand of God. Set your minds on things that are above, not on things that are on earth. For you have died, and your life is hid with Christ in God. When Christ who is our life appears, then you also will appear with him in glory. (Col 3:1-4 RSV)*

- Be free from concerns and free from cares of this world, as evidence of our trust in God: *Therefore I [Christ] tell you, do not be anxious about your life, (Matt 6:25 RSV).* When we are free of the cares of this world, then we can have an undivided devotion to God. (I Cor 7:35 RSV)

- Have the mind of Christ which is to be servant of all: *Have this mind among yourselves, which is yours in Christ Jesus, who, though he was in the form of God, did not count equality with God a thing to be grasped, but emptied himself, taking the form of a servant, being born in the likeness of men. And being found in human form he humbled himself and became obedient unto death, even death on a cross. Therefore God has highly exalted him and bestowed on him the name which is above every name, that at the name of Jesus every knee should bow, in heaven and on earth and under the earth, and every tongue confess that Jesus Christ is Lord, to the glory of God the Father. (Phil 2:5-11 RSV)*

- Fix our eyes on Jesus: *Therefore, since we are surrounded by so great a cloud of witnesses, let us also lay aside every weight, and sin which clings so closely, and let us run with perseverance the race that is set before us, looking to Jesus the pioneer and perfecter of our faith, who for the joy that was set before him endured the cross, despising the shame, and is seated at the right hand of the throne of God. Consider him who endured from sinners such hostility against himself, so that you may not grow weary or fainthearted. (Heb 12:1-3 RSV)*

- To know the power and purpose of prayer which is to unite us in divine conversation with God our Father.

- The importance of baptism: *I [John the Baptist] baptize you with water for repentance, but he who is coming after me is mightier than I, whose sandals I am not worthy to carry; he will baptize you with the Holy Spirit and with fire. (Matt 3:11 RSV)*

- The importance of baptism lies in the fact that the Holy Spirit is given at that sacrament (see Baptism of Christ: John 1:33 RSV; Acts 2:38 RSV).
- The certainty of the resurrection and eternal life: *Jesus said to her, "I am the resurrection and the life; he who believes in me, though he die, yet shall he live, and whoever lives and believes in me shall never die. Do you believe this?" She said to him, "Yes, Lord; I believe that you are the Christ, the Son of God, he who is coming into the world." (John 11:25-27 RSV)*

Above all, we must teach the gospel message. We are to bring people to Christ so that He can save them. (Luke 19:10)

We are to make disciples by the manner in which we live, by the degree to which we love and trust God, by the degree to which we love one another, by the degree to which we serve one another, and by the degree to which we witness to the world about Christ, our Savior and our Lord.

Go therefore and make disciples of all nations (Matt 28:19 RSV)

Because of Love, He came …

Chapter 32. I have come to bring fire on the earth (Luke 12:49)

I have come to bring fire on the earth, and how I wish it were already kindled! But I have a baptism to undergo, and how distressed I am until it is completed! Do you think I came to bring peace on earth? No, I tell you, but division. (Luke 12:49-51)

By day the LORD went ahead of them in a pillar of cloud to guide them on their way and by night in a pillar of fire to give them light, so that they could travel by day or night. Neither the pillar of cloud by day nor the pillar of fire by night left its place in front of the people. (Ex 13:21-22)

To the Israelites the glory of the LORD looked like a consuming fire on top of the mountain. (Ex 24:17)

I [John the Baptist] baptize you with water for repentance. But after me will come one who is more powerful than I, whose sandals I am not fit to carry. He will baptize you with the Holy Spirit and with fire. (Matt 3:11-12)

This is a uniquely important reason for the birth of Christ.

In this passage, Jesus is talking about three events: *first, bringing fire on the earth; second, Christ has a baptism to undergo; third, He came to bring division, not peace.*

So, let's see what each of these mean and their significance for His Incarnation.

First, Christ has come to bring *fire* to the earth. It is certain that He is not speaking literally; the earth already has fire in a physical sense. What kind of *fire* is He talking about?

179

In the Scriptures, *fire* is a symbol of God's Presence, His Power, and His judgment. Fire is also indicative of God's leading His people, physically (in the wilderness) and spiritually. *Fire* is also indicative of the fact that God has accepted the sacrifice of His people.

In the final days, fire from heaven is the instrument of God's wrath to crush the rebellion of Satan and leads to Satan being thrown into the lake of burning sulfur, where the beast and the false prophet had been thrown.

When the thousand years are over, Satan will be released from his prison and will go out to deceive the nations in the four corners of the earth — Gog and Magog — to gather them for battle. In number they are like the sand on the seashore. They marched across the breadth of the earth and surrounded the camp of God's people, the city he loves. But fire came down from heaven and devoured them. And the devil, who deceived them, was thrown into the lake of burning sulfur, where the beast and the false prophet had been thrown. They will be tormented day and night forever and ever. (Rev 20:7-10)

So, it seems clear that the *fire* which Christ will bring to the earth is God's presence, His love, His power, His judgment, His provision, and His protection. God is an all-consuming fire to awaken His people to return to Him, to love Him, and to be faithful and obedient to Him. That is the purpose of the *fire* that Christ will bring to earth.

Second, Christ said that He had a *baptism* to undergo. What could He mean by this unusual statement? Now, baptism also indicates both the sign and the seal of entering into a covenant between God and man. On God's part, the covenant is God's pledge to forgive and save man. Because of what He has done and what He has promised, God forgives the repentant and regenerates the individual by transforming a sinner into the righteousness of God. On the one hand, baptism is a sign of that covenant in Jeremiah 31:31-34. On the other, it is the means by which people enter into that covenant.

So, if Christ has a *baptism* to undergo, then it must be so that the covenant (Jeremiah 31:31-34) for the forgiveness of sins can be ratified which means that the shedding of blood must occur. Christ's blood will be shed on the cross, and so the baptism that He must undergo in His death on the cross. He is pointing to the cross; that is His *baptism.*

Third, He said that He came to bring *division,* not *peace.* Why division? Why not peace? Peace is redemption and reconciliation with God. Division implies a separation of that which was united. However, if the people were united to pagan influence, and if the people were united in acts of disobedience, rebellion, and being stiff-necked, then God said that they need to be separated from that type of behavior.

So Jesus Christ is coming to separate evil from the things of God, so that the things of God will be those standards to which the people are united.

They need to be *separated from* evil so that they can be *united to* good.

So Christ came to bring fire to the earth, to undergo a baptism, and to bring division, not peace.

Such was necessary to establish the Kingdom that God had always intended to be in His Creation.

This could only be accomplished through the Incarnation.

I have come to bring fire on the earth (Luke 12:49)

Because of Love, He came …

Chapter 33. For judgment I have come into this world (John 9:39)

*Jesus said, "**For judgment I have come into this world**, so that the blind will see and those who see will become blind." (John 9:39)*

This represents another unusual reason for the birth of Jesus Christ.

Jesus now made a resounding statement regarding judgment. To do so, He separated mankind into two categories: those that *see* and those who are *blind*. However, He might be talking more about the relationship between *darkness* and *light*. We shall see how this unfolds.

We will also see here a separation between the physical and the spiritual sense of being *blind*.

Those who *see* are in the light; those who are *blind* are in darkness.

Christ most likely was speaking of *seeing* and being *blind* in a spiritual sense—not in a physical sense.

This text might be expressed this way: *I [Christ] came to declare the condition of men; to show them their responsibility and the danger associated with their present conduct. My coming will mean that some will be justified, redeemed, and saved, while others will face God's wrath and His condemnation.*

However, Jesus Christ is present, not as a preacher in the pulpit, but as a king upon the throne and a judge upon the bench.

Now, in those capacities, He is talking about judgment on those who are blind and those who see-- those in darkness and those in the light.

Why these limited categories? What is the significance? Let's see where the Scriptures lead us.

We begin by recognizing that *blindness* can be either physical or spiritual; we also recognize that we *see*, either physically or spiritually.

The Old Testament contains many truths regarding the spiritually blind, as those who have sinned against the Lord.

I will bring distress on the people and they will walk like blind men, because they have sinned against the LORD. (Zeph 1:17)

In this passage, the blind are those who are sinners.

Lead out those who have eyes but are blind, who have ears but are deaf. (Isa 43:8)

All who make idols are nothing, and the things they treasure are worthless. Those who would speak up for them are blind; they are ignorant, to their own shame. (Isa 44:9)

Then the disciples came to him and asked, "Do you know that the Pharisees were offended when they heard this?" He replied, "Every plant that my heavenly Father has not planted will be pulled up by the roots. Leave them; they are blind guides. If a blind man leads a blind man, both will fall into a pit." (Matt 15:12-14)

However, if we consider the spiritual aspect of His statement, the *blind* are most likely those who have eyes but are spiritually blind: they are those who pray to idols, who have sinned against the Lord, and who are in spiritual darkness.

Those who *see* are in the light because they are obedient to the will of God.

So, His condemnation is for those in *darkness* in contrast to those in the *light*. Those in darkness can see physically; however, they are *spiritually blind*.

In addition, it is also possible that He is referring to those who believe that they are in the light, while, in reality, they are in darkness.

So, it appears that Christ is talking about two types of people: those in *darkness* and those in the *light*.

First, what does *darkness* imply?

Since darkness was associated with the conditions that existed before the creation, it is associated with evil, which will lead to God's wrath and His condemnation (Job 17:12; 21:17). Darkness is also equated with death. In Sheol, the land of the dead, there is only darkness (Job

10:21-22; 38:17). Further, darkness symbolizes man's ignorance of God's will and, therefore, it is associated with sin (Job 24:13-17).

Darkness also describes the condition of those who have not yet seen the light of Christ (John 1:4-5; 12:35; Eph 5:14) and those who deliberately turn away from the light (John 3:19-20). Hating the light brings God's condemnation (Col 1:13; 2 Peter 2:17). Living in darkness describes those who have not repented (Rev 16:10; 18:23). In addition, darkness symbolizes error, evil, and the works of Satan (Gen 1:4).

The apostle John understood the difference between light and darkness as did the prophet Isaiah.

This is the verdict: Light has come into the world, but men loved darkness instead of light because their deeds were evil. Everyone who does evil hates the light, and will not come into the light for fear that his deeds will be exposed. But whoever lives by the truth comes into the light, so that it may be seen plainly that what he has done has been done through God. (John 3:19-21)

The people walking in darkness have seen a great light; on those living in the land of the shadow of death a light has dawned. (Isa 9:2; Matt 4:16)

Those who are blind spiritually have not seen the great Light, Jesus Christ,

Conversely, what does *light* imply?

In the Scriptures, light symbolizes God's presence, His truth, His holiness, His purity, and His righteous and redemptive activities. The Scriptures also refer to God as the light to guide His obedient people.

God is light (1 John 1:5); when we walk in the light, we shall be purified from all sin.

This is the message we have heard from him and declare to you: God is light; in him there is no darkness at all. If we claim to have fellowship with him yet walk in the darkness, we lie and do not live by the truth. But if we walk in the light, as he is in the light, we have fellowship with one another, and the blood of Jesus, his Son, purifies us from all sin. (1 John 1:5-7)

The Psalms declare: *The Lord is my light and my salvation; whom shall I fear? (Ps 27:1)*

God's Word, the Bible, is a lamp to guide the believer. *Your word is a lamp to my feet and a light to my path. (Psa 119:105)*

Finally, the Scriptures identify Jesus Christ as the divine illumination:

I am the light of the world (John 8:12). Because of who He is, those who rejected this divine light would bring *judgment* upon themselves. (John 3:19-21)

> When Jesus spoke again to the people, he said, "I am the light of the world. Whoever follows me will never walk in darkness, but will have the light of life." (John 8:12)

As Jesus Christ is the Light of the world, Christians are called to be *the light of the world* (Matt 5:14).

> You [Christians] are the light of the world. A city on a hill cannot be hidden. Neither do people light a lamp and put it under a bowl. Instead they put it on its stand, and it gives light to everyone in the house. In the same way, let your light shine before men, that they may see your good deeds and praise your Father in heaven. (Matt 5:14-16)

So we have this comparison between those who are *in darkness* and those in the *light*. We should understand that darkness and light are consistent with those who are *blind* and those who *see*.

Jesus addressed this subject Himself when, in the synagogue at Nazareth, He read from the prophet, Isaiah: *He said, "[God] has anointed me to preach the gospel to the poor. He has sent me to heal the brokenhearted, to preach deliverance to the captives, and recovery of sight to the blind." (Luke 4:18)*.

Consider this short but most meaningful passage: see how God has sent His Son and *anointed me* [Christ] for four purposes: *first, to preach the gospel; second, to heal the brokenhearted; third, to preach deliverance to the captives, and, fourth, recovering of sight to the blind.*

So, since Christ is talking about *blind* and *seeing*, about darkness and light, we can expect that this New Testament message has its roots in the Old Testament. God had always dealt with a people who heard, but did not understand; who saw, but never perceived.

> He said, "Go and tell this people: 'Be ever hearing, but never understanding; be ever seeing, but never perceiving.' Make the heart of this people calloused; make their ears dull and close their eyes. Otherwise they might see with their eyes, hear with their ears, understand with their hearts, and turn and be healed." (Isa 6:9-10)

This passage is so important that it is repeated three times in the New Testament: Matthew 13:14, Mark 4:12, and Acts 28:26.

In addition, Christ is talking about judgment on those who are blind and those who see.

What is *judgment* and what is implied in this case?

Divine judgment is based on both the Person of God and the Laws of God. Judgment means the investigation of facts, the application of truth, and the rendering of a verdict, which would lead to justification or to condemnation. Justification means that the individual had been declared innocent, pardoned, and set free. Condemnation means that the wrath of God would rest on the individual and that eternal separation from God would result.

Jesus said, "For judgment I have come into this world, so that the blind will see and those who see will become blind." (John 9:39)

So Jesus has come so that the blind will see and that those who see will become blind.

This statement means that Christ wants those in spiritual darkness to come into the Light and receive the salvation for which He died. Conversely, Christ wants those who *see* to become *blind*, because they reject Him as the Son of God, the Messiah, the Christ. Such is God's Judgment on the world.

Salvation awaits those who live in the Light; condemnation awaits those who reject the Christ.

For judgment I have come into this world (John 9:39)

Because of Love, He came ...

Chapter 34. The reason the Son of God appeared was to destroy the devil's work (1 John 3:8)

He who does what is sinful is of the devil, because the devil has been sinning from the beginning. **The reason the Son of God appeared was to destroy the devil's work.** *(1 John 3:8)*

… how God anointed Jesus of Nazareth with the Holy Spirit and power, and how he went around doing good and healing all who were under the power of the devil, because God was with him. (Acts 10:38)

Submit yourselves, then, to God. Resist the devil, and he will flee from you. Come near to God and he will come near to you. (James 4:7-8)

Here we have a vital reason for the Incarnation: to destroy the devil's work.

Notice that Christ has come to destroy the works of the devil; it is not to destroy the devil himself: that will occur at the end of the age when Satan, the antichrist, and the false prophet are thrown into the lake of fire. (Rev 20:14-15)

Christ's purpose was the destruction of the work of the devil.

Accordingly, it is important to understand who the devil is: Satan, the great deceiver, the liar, and the enemy of God and man. The name, Satan, appears 53 times in both the Old and New Testaments, while the term, devil, occurs 33 times and that only in the New Testament. Satan, the devil, means the tempter (1 Thess 3:5); Beelzebub (Matt 12:24); the wicked one (Matt 13:19,38); the ruler of this world (John

12:31); the god of this age (2 Cor 4:4); Belial (2 Cor 6:15), the prince of the power of the air (Eph 2:2); and the accuser of our brethren (Rev 12:10). The devil is a liar and the father of lies.

You [Jews] who would not believe in Christ belong to your father, the devil, and you want to carry out your father's desire. He was a murderer from the beginning, not holding to the truth, for there is no truth in him. When he lies, he speaks his native language, for he is a liar and the father of lies. (John 8:44)

The origin of Satan, the devil, is generally believed to rest on two biblical passages, Isaiah 14:12-15 and Ezekiel 28:11-19, which relate to his ambition, his removal from heaven, and his goals in the world.

Satan's primary ambition was/is to replace God and have the world worship him (Matt 4:8-9; Rev 13:4, 12).

Consider the temptations of Jesus in the wilderness (Matt 4:1-11). This passage begins with a most unusual statement. *Then Jesus was led by the Spirit into the desert to be tempted by the devil. (Matt 4:1)* How can Jesus be led by the Spirit and tempted by the devil *at the same time?* However, that is a mark of the Christian life; we too will be led by the Spirit and tempted by the devil; it will always be so.

Next, consider how the devil tried to encourage everyone, including Jesus, to worship him. Satan tempts everyone with lies, masquerading as the truth.

Again, the devil took him to a very high mountain and showed him all the kingdoms of the world and their splendor. "All this I will give you," he said, *"if you will bow down and worship me." Jesus said to him, "Away from me, Satan! For it is written: 'Worship the Lord your God, and serve him only.'" (Matt 4:8-10)*

The interesting message in this dialogue is the following: *Through him all things were made; without him nothing was made that has been made. (John 1:3)* The kingdoms belonged to Jesus; they were His; they did not belong to the devil, and the devil had no right to offer or to give.

We must recognize Satan as *the wicked one (Matt 13:19, 38),* while God is *the Holy One (Isa 1:4).* Satan is the one who sows destruction in the world. Consider the parable by Jesus regarding the good seed and the bad seed. *The field is the world, and the good seed stands for the sons of the kingdom. The weeds are the sons of the evil one, and the enemy who sows them is the devil. The harvest is the end of the age, and the harvesters are angels. As the weeds are pulled up and burned in the fire, so it will be at the end of the age. The Son of Man will send out his angels, and they will weed out of his kingdom everything that causes sin and all who do evil. They will throw them into the fiery furnace, where there will be weeping and gnashing of teeth. Then the righteous will shine like the sun in the kingdom of their Father. He who has ears, let him hear.* (Matt 13:38-43)

Satan brought sin into the human family (Gen 3); Satan has gained the power of death--a power which Christ has broken through His crucifixion and resurrection.

Since the children [those whom God had given Christ] have flesh and blood, he [Christ] too shared in their humanity so that by his death he might destroy him who holds the power of death — that is, the devil — and free those who all their lives were held in slavery by their fear of death. (Heb 2:14-15)

Satan uses various methods to achieve his goal; the principal ones are temptation (Matt 4:3; 1 Thess 3:5) and deception *(1 Tim 3:6-7; 2 Tim 2:26).*

His lying nature stands in bold contrast to the truth for which Christ stands (John 8:32, 44). Satan, the great deceiver, falsifies the truth (2 Cor 11:13-15).

Satan's goals are to separate people from the truth of God and to silence the gospel. He seeks to stop the spread of God's Word (Matt 13:19; 1 Thess 2:17-18).

Whenever the gospel is preached, Satan tries to blind people's understanding so they cannot grasp the meaning of the message (2 Cor 4:3-4; 2 Thess 2:9-10).

At times he opposes the work of God by violent means (John 13:2, 27; 1 Peter 5:8; Rev 12:13-17).

He brings disorder into the physical world by afflicting and tempting human beings (Job 1-2; 2 Cor 12:7; Heb 2:14). His continuing work of evil is described in Revelation 12, in which Satan tries to destroy Christ (Rev 12:4-5). However, during the tribulation before Christ's Second Coming, Satan will be cast out of heaven (Rev 12:7-12);

he will be bound for a thousand years before finally being cast into the lake of fire (Rev 20:2, 10).

The Cross of Christ is the basis for Satan's final defeat (Heb 2:14-15; 1 Peter 3:18, 22). The final victory will occur when Jesus returns and Satan is cast into the lake of fire.

The great dragon was hurled down — that ancient serpent called the devil, or Satan, who leads the whole world astray. He was hurled to the earth, and his angels with him. And the devil, who deceived them, was thrown into the lake of burning sulfur, where the beast and the false prophet had been thrown. They will be tormented day and night forever and ever. (Rev 20:9-10)

In all encounters with the devil, the advice to every believer is this:

Be self-controlled and alert. Your enemy the devil prowls around like a roaring lion looking for someone to devour. Resist him, standing firm in the faith, because you know that your brothers throughout the world are undergoing the same kind of sufferings. And the God of all grace, who called you to his eternal glory in Christ, after you have suffered a little while, will himself restore you and make you strong, firm and steadfast. To him be the power forever and ever. Amen. (1 Peter 5:8-11)

The works of the devil which Jesus Christ came to destroy are *his attempts to separate believers from God, his temptations, his deception, his calling a lie the truth, his opposition to Christ and the gospel and the Kingdom of God.*

I close this chapter by reminding the reader of Matthew 6:13, a petition in the Lord's Prayer.

And lead us not into temptation, but deliver us from the evil one. (Matt 6:13)

Some might misunderstand and think: we are asking God that He would not lead us into temptation. That is clearly not the sense of the passage. Therefore, the text should more accurately read: *lead us through temptation; deliver us from the evil one.*

That is what we seek in any encounter with the devil. When tempted, God, lead us through temptation.

God, deliver us from the evil one.

Christ, thank you for coming to destroy the works of the devil.

Because of Love, He came …

The reason the Son of God appeared was to destroy the devil's work (1 John 3:8)

Because of Love, He came …

Chapter 35. See, I have told you ahead of time. (Matt 24:25)

The Sign of your Coming and the End of the Age (Matt 24:1-44; Mark 13:3-36; Luke 21:7-36)

*Jesus left the temple and was walking away when his disciples came up to him to call his attention to its buildings. "Do you see all these things?" he asked. "I tell you the truth, not one stone here will be left on another; everyone will be thrown down." As Jesus was sitting on the Mount of Olives, the disciples came to him privately. "Tell us," they said, "when will this happen, and what will be the **sign of your coming and of the end of the age?**" Jesus answered: "Watch out that no one deceives you. For many will come in my name, claiming, 'I am the Christ,' and will deceive many. You will hear of wars and rumors of wars, but see to it that you are not alarmed. Such things must happen, but the end is still to come. Nation will rise against nation, and kingdom against kingdom. There will be famines and earthquakes in various places. All these are the beginning of birth pains." (Matt 24:1-8)*

See, I [Christ] have told you ahead of time. (Matt 24:25)

We now have before us a most important reason for the Incarnation: this is to explain what must happen before the Second Coming of Christ and the events which must occur at the end of the age.

This great message to the world would not have been possible without the Incarnation.

Now, many of the great questions of the Scriptures are centered around the signs of the end of this age and Christ's Second Coming.

The message describing the end of the age, as given in Matthew 24:1-44, is also outlined in Mark 13 and Luke 21.

"Tell us," they [His disciples] said, "when will this happen, and what will be the sign of your coming and of the end of the age?"

The Scriptures state that Christ's future return to the earth will occur at the end of the present age. Although the Bible explicitly speaks of Christ's appearance as a *second time*, the phrase *second coming* occurs nowhere in the New Testament. Many passages, however, speak of His return. In fact, in the New Testament alone, it is referred to over 300 times.

The night before His crucifixion, Jesus confirmed that He would return. (John 14:3).

And if I [Christ] go and prepare a place for you [my disciples], I will come back and take you to be with me that you also may be where I am. (John 14:3)

After His crucifixion, death, burial, and resurrection, Christ appeared to many of His disciples.

For what I [Paul] received I passed on to you as of first importance: that Christ died for our sins according to the Scriptures, that he was buried, that he was raised on the third day according to the Scriptures, and that he appeared to Peter, and then to the Twelve. After that, he appeared to more than five hundred of the brothers at the same time, most of whom are still living, though some have fallen asleep. Then he appeared to James, then to all the apostles, and last of all he appeared to me also, as to one abnormally born. (1 Cor 15:3-8)

When Jesus ascended into heaven, two angels appeared to His followers, saying that He would return in the same manner as they had seen Him go (Acts 1:11). The New Testament is filled with expectancy of His return, even as Christians are today.

They [the disciples] were looking intently up into the sky as he [Christ] was going, when suddenly two men dressed in white stood beside them. "Men of Galilee," they said, "why do you stand here looking into the sky? This same Jesus, who has been taken from you into heaven, will come back in the same way you have seen him go into heaven." (Acts 1:10-11)

So the Ascension and the Second Coming of Christ are well-documented divine events in the plan of God. However, various opinions exist about what is meant by the Second Coming. Some regard it as the coming of the Holy Spirit on the day of Pentecost. Others regard it as the coming of Christ into the heart at conversion. Christ's coming for the believer at the time of death is still another view.

Careful examination of the New Testament, however, makes it clear that the Second Coming will be a climactic historical event. The Lord will return in the same manner in which He left. His coming will be personal, bodily, and visible.

The time of the Second Coming is unknown: in fact, Jesus stated that only the Father knows the time. Therefore, the return of the Lord should be a matter of constant expectancy. As He came the first time, in the *fullness of time (Gal 4:4),* so will the Second Coming be. The believer's task is not to try to determine the time of the Second Coming. Instead, we must share the gospel message with great energy and enthusiasm until He returns (Acts 1:8-11).

A companion to the Second Coming is the general context of the End of the Age. There is no subject as controversial as this. The debates rage over the character of the Millennium, the return of Christ, and the order and sequence in which the events describing the End of the Age will occur.

Perhaps the greatest theological uncertainty, and thereby debate, is that associated with the understanding of the relationship of the Millennium and the Second Coming of Christ.

To begin with, the Millennium is considered that thousand-year period mentioned in connection with the description of Christ's coming to reign with His saints over the earth (Rev 19:11-16; 20:1-9). Many Old Testament passages refer to the millennium (Isa 11:4; Jer 3:17; Zech 14:9).

But do not forget this one thing, dear friends: With the Lord a day is like a thousand years, and a thousand years are like a day. (2 Peter 3:8)

So regardless of how this Millennium period is seen, it represents that period in which Satan will be bound in the bottomless pit before his short period of release (Rev 20:3, 7-8). During this time, the faithful martyrs will be resurrected. They will rule with Christ and will be priests of God and Christ (Rev 5:10; 20:4). The unbelieving dead will wait for the second resurrection (Rev 20:5). After the Millennium, Satan will be released to resume his work of lies and deception (Rev 20:7-8).

The most important aspect of the Millennium is the reign of Christ.

In Peter's speech at the first Christian Pentecost, he taught that Christ now rules from the right hand of God (Acts 2:33-36). That rule will last until His enemies are made His footstool (Ps 110:1). The apostle Paul also understood Christ to be presently reigning in a period designed to bring all of God's enemies underfoot (1 Cor 15:25-27). Therefore, the impact of Christ's present rule over the earth from God's right hand must be seen as completely related to His future reign during the Millennium. The Millennium is viewed by interpreters in several different ways. One position holds that the Millennium refers to Christ's spiritual rule today from heaven. This symbolic view is known as the *amillennial* interpretation. Another position views Christ's spiritual rule as working through preaching and teaching to bring gradual world improvement leading up to Christ's return. This is the *postmillennial* view. The position that holds to an actual thousand year period in the future is known as the *premillennial* view. This interpretation does not diminish the power of Christ's present rule from heaven or limit that rule to the church only.

So we begin.

The end is not to be expected instantly. There are still signs to come to pass (2 Thess 2:3); the number of martyrs must be filled (Rev 6:11). There is need of patience (James 5:7), but it is at hand (1 Peter 4:7; Rev 1:3; 22:10). *Yet a little while* (Heb 10:37, 25), *The night is far spent* (Rom 13:12), *The Lord is at hand* (Phil 4:5). *We who are alive* expect to see it (1 Thess 4:15; 1 Cor 15:51); the time is short (1 Cor 7:29). Indeed, there is hardly time for repentance (Rev 22:11), and being alert and watchful is demanded (1 Thess 5:6; Rev 3:3).

An outpouring of the Spirit is a sign of the end (Acts 2:17-18). But the world is growing steadily worse; for the godly, intense trials are coming, although those especially favored may be spared suffering (Rev 3:10). This is the beginning of Judgment (1 Peter 4:17). Iniquity increases and false teachers are multiplied (Jude verse 18; 2 Peter 3:3; 2 Tim 3:1). Above all there is to be an outburst of evil through the efforts of the antichrist (I John 2:18, 22; 4:3; 2 John 7; 2 Thess 2:8-10; Rev 19:19), who will seek to gather all nations (Rev 19:19; 2 Thess 2:10). Plagues will occur (Rev 9:18), and the conversion of the Jews (Rom 11:26) will result from these plagues (Rev 11:13). Then Christ is manifested and Antichrist is slain (2 Thess 2:8; Rev 19:20). The general resurrection follows.

First, an outpouring of the Spirit is considered the initial sign of the end of the Age (Acts 2:17-18).

Second, during this time, the world is growing steadily hostile to the godly, and the saints are severely tested. Faith will be tested; evil, greater than ever seen, will dominate the world.

Third, then the judgment will begin (1 Peter 4:17).

Fourth, iniquity will increase, and false teachers will multiply (Jude 18; 2 Peter 3:3; 2 Tim 3:13).

Fifth, the antichrist will emerge (I John 2:18, 22; 4:3; 2 John 7; 2 Thess 2:8-10; Rev 19:19), and he will attempt to assemble all nations under his banner (Rev 19:19; 2 Thess 2:10).

Sixth, plagues will fall upon all men, and natural disasters will occur (Acts 2:19-20). There will be wars and rumors of wars (Matt 24:6).

These plagues (Rev 11:13) will lead to the conversion of the Jews (Rom 11:26).

At this point, Christ returns and is manifest: with His return, the antichrist is slain (2 Thess 2:8; Rev 19:20).

Then the Millennium begins (Rev 20:3) leading to the general resurrection of saints and sinners.

This general and total resurrection leads to the Final Judgment.

This chapter is going to be more personal than any other chapter that I have written in this book or in my other books. I have tried to restrict my personal views, but I believe that I cannot do it on this subject. So permit me this one exception.

Let me tell what I do know and what I don't know.

I know that there will be a Day of the Lord.

Wail, for the day of the LORD is near; it will come like destruction from the Almighty. (Isa 13:6)

In the last days, God says, I will pour out my Spirit on all people. Your sons and daughters will prophesy, your young men will see visions, your old men will dream dreams. Even on my servants, both men and women, I will pour out my Spirit in those days, and they will prophesy. I will show wonders in the heaven above and signs on the earth below, blood and fire and billows of smoke. The sun will be turned to darkness and the moon to blood before the coming of the great and glorious day of the Lord. And everyone who calls on the name of the Lord will be saved. (Acts 2:17-21; Joel 2:28-32)

I know that we will stand before the Great White Throne.

Then I saw a great white throne and him who was seated on it. Earth and sky fled from his presence, and there was no place for them. And I saw the dead, great and small, standing before the throne, and books were opened. Another book was opened, which is the book of life. (Rev 20:11-12)

I know that there will be a Final Judgment.

Then I saw another angel flying in midair, and he had the eternal gospel to proclaim to those who live on the earth — to every nation, tribe, language and people. He said in a loud voice, "Fear God and give him glory, because the hour of his judgment has come. Worship him who made the heavens, the earth, the sea and the springs of water." (Rev 14:6-7)

Now we know that God's judgment against those who do such things is based on truth. So when you, a mere man, pass judgment on them and yet do the same things, do you think you will escape God's judgment ? Or do you show contempt for the riches of his kindness, tolerance and patience, not realizing that God's kindness leads you toward repentance? But because of your stubbornness and your unrepentant heart, you are storing up wrath against yourself for the day of God's wrath, when his righteous judgment will be revealed. God "will give to each person according to what he has done." To those who by persistence in doing good seek glory, honor and immortality, he will give eternal life. But for those who are self-seeking and who reject the truth and follow evil, there will be wrath and anger. There will be trouble and distress for every human being who does evil: first for the Jew, then for the Gentile; but glory, honor and peace for everyone who does good: first for the Jew, then for the Gentile. For God does not show favoritism. (Rom 2:2-11)

I know that there will be a Great Tribulation.

All the angels were standing around the throne and around the elders and the four living creatures. They fell down on their faces before the throne and worshiped God, saying: "Amen! Praise and glory and wisdom and thanks and honor and power and strength be to our God forever and ever. Amen!"

Then one of the elders asked me, "These in white robes — who are they, and where did they come from?" I answered, "Sir, you know." And he said, "These are they who have come out of the great tribulation; they have washed their robes and made them white in the blood of the Lamb. Therefore, "they are before the throne of God and serve him day and night in his temple; and he who sits on the throne will spread his tent over them. Never again will they hunger; never again will they thirst. The sun will not beat upon them, nor any scorching heat. For the Lamb at the center of the throne will be their shepherd; he will lead them to springs of living water. And God will wipe away every tear from their eyes." (Rev 7:11-17)

I know that there will be the Second Coming of Christ.

I know that there will be a Millennium.

I know that there will be a resurrection.

I know that He will make all things new (Rev 21:5).

I know that He is coming soon (Rev 22:7).

I know that there will be a new Heaven and a New Earth

I know that there will be a New Jerusalem, the new city of God, the new *ekklesia* of God.

I know that God has a grand plan for a new Creation.

I know that I will spend eternity with Him.

Here is what I don't know.

I don't know when these events will occur.

I don't know the order or sequence when these will occur.

God has told me what He wants me to know; He has not told me what I don't need to know.

Christ has told us that even He does not know the day or the time. If He does not know, why do I think that I need to know something that even the Son of God does not know?

Instead, Christ has told you and me to be prepared for God's plan for the renewal of His Creation.

What if God, choosing to show his wrath and make his power known, bore with great patience the objects of his wrath — prepared for destruction? What if he did this to make the riches of his glory known to the objects of his mercy, whom he prepared in advance for glory— even us, whom he also called, not only from the Jews but also from the Gentiles? As he says in Hosea: "I will call them 'my people' who are not my people; and I will call her 'my loved one' who is not my loved one," (Rom 9:22-25)

Instead, they were longing for a better country — a heavenly one. Therefore God is not ashamed to be called their God, for he has prepared a city for them. (Heb 11:16)

Therefore keep watch, because you do not know on what day your Lord will come. (Matt 24:42-43)

Be on guard! Be alert! You do not know when that time will come. (Mark 13:33-34)

Christ has told me that He will make all things new.

Then I saw a new heaven and a new earth, for the first heaven and the first earth had passed away, and there was no longer any sea. I saw the Holy City, the new Jerusalem, coming down out of heaven from God, prepared as a bride beautifully dressed for her husband. And I heard a loud voice from the throne saying, "Now the dwelling of God is with men, and he will live with them. They will be his people, and God himself will be with them and be their God. He will wipe every tear from their eyes. There will be no more death or mourning or crying or pain, for the old order of things has passed away." He who was seated on the throne said, "I am making everything new!" Then he said, "Write this down, for these words are trustworthy and true." (Rev 21:1-5)

I don't need to worry about it; I don't need to be anxious about it; I just need to be ready for whatever God has for His new creation. For me, I don't need to know every detail; I know that He has promised and that is sufficient for me.

See, I have told you ahead of time. (Matt 24:25)

Because of Love, He came ...

Part III. Epilogue

Chapter 36. Summary

For God so loved the world that he gave his one and only Son, that whoever believes in him shall not perish but have eternal life. For God did not send his Son into the world to condemn the world, but to save the world through him. Whoever believes in him is not condemned, but whoever does not believe stands condemned already because he has not believed in the name of God's one and only Son. This is the verdict: Light has come into the world, but men loved darkness instead of light because their deeds were evil. Everyone who does evil hates the light, and will not come into the light for fear that his deeds will be exposed. But whoever lives by the truth comes into the light, so that it may be seen plainly that what he has done has been done through God. (John 3:16-21)

The Incarnation of Jesus Christ is one of the great moments in divine history. It is the demonstration of God's great love; it is the foundation for the Fatherhood of God; it is the moment which predestines the Cross of Christ.

Therefore, it is appropriate that such a momentous event be thoroughly studied and understood.

We began this examination by considering the foundational theology which is *The Love of God; Christ, the Son of God;* and *The Cross of Christ.* From that theology, we learned these truths:

He came because of the love of God.

God came in the flesh as His only begotten Son.

The Savior of the world is God Himself.

He came to redeem sinners and reconcile them to God.

He came to save you and me.

He came to bring light into the darkness of this evil age.

He was rejected, and we esteemed Him not.

He came to die on a cross, reserved for criminals.

His cross is a witness to the love of God; His cross is the basis of our salvation.

His cross is the basis of our righteousness; His cross is the basis of the forgiveness of our sins; His cross is the basis of our peace with God.

In this study of the Incarnation, 30 reasons were presented which provide direct and indirect reasons for the Incarnation.

The direct reasons are based on the 12 statements in which Jesus Christ said: *I have come ...*

Do not think that I have come to abolish the Law or the Prophets; I have not come to abolish them but to fulfill them. (Matt 5:17)

Do not suppose that I have come to bring peace to the earth. I did not come to bring peace, but a sword. For I have come to turn 'a man against his father, a daughter against her mother, a daughter-in-law against her mother-in-law— a man's enemies will be the members of his own household.' (Matt 10:34-36)

Jesus replied, "Let us go somewhere else — to the nearby villages — so I can preach there also. That is why I have come." (Mark 1:38)

I have come to bring fire on the earth, and how I wish it were already kindled! (Luke 12:49)

I have come in my Father's name, and you do not accept me; but if someone else comes in his own name, you will accept him. (John 5:43)

For I have come down from heaven not to do my will but to do the will of him who sent me. (John 6:38)

Jesus said, "For judgment I have come into this world, so that the blind will see and those who see will become blind." (John 9:39)

The thief comes only to steal and kill and destroy; I have come that they may have life, and have it to the full. (John 10:10)

I have come into the world as a light, so that no one who believes in me should stay in darkness. (John 12:46)

Therefore, when Christ came into the world, he said: "Sacrifice and offering you did not desire, but a body you prepared for me; with burnt offerings and sin offerings you were not pleased. Then I said, 'Here I am — it is written about me in the scroll —I have come to do your will, O God." *(Heb 10:5-7)*

In these passages, Christ said: *I had come* for the following reasons: to witness to God, the Father; to bring the message and means of salvation; to fulfill the Scriptures; and to impact the world for the Kingdom of God.

In addition to these passages, the trial of Jesus Christ before Pilate, the Roman Procurator of Judea, adds an additional reason for His Incarnation.

"You are a king, then!" said Pilate. Jesus answered, "You are right in saying I am a king. In fact, for this reason I was born, and for this I came into the world, to testify to the truth. Everyone on the side of truth listens to me." (John 18:37)

Christ, the King, came *to testify to the truth.*

Now, looking at these 30 reasons, it seemed appropriate to group them into four areas: *God, Salvation, the Scriptures, and the World.*

The combined reasons reveal to the world the love and heart of God. These reasons present us with many great truths, such as the following:

Christ came in His Father's name and to do the Father's will.

Christ came to reveal the Father: if you have seen me, you have seen the Father.

Christ came to preach the good news of the Kingdom of God.

Christ came to reveal and send another Counselor, the Spirit of God.

Christ came to give glory to His Father.

Christ came that we would become the children of God.

Christ came to give us life.

Christ came to save sinners.

Christ came to lay down His life for the sheep.

Christ came to die according to the Scriptures.

Christ came to call sinners to repentance.

Christ came to preach good news to the poor.

Christ came to rescue us from the present evil age.

Christ came to teach us to pray.

Christ came to identify His disciples.

Christ came to make us a new creation.

Christ came to fulfill the Law and the Prophets.

Christ came to fulfill the Scriptures.

Christ came to be a light in the world.

Christ came to testify to the truth.

Christ came to build His church.

Christ came to equip His disciples to go into all the world and make disciples.

Christ came to bring fire on the earth.

Christ came to bring judgment to the world.

Christ came to destroy the works of the devil.

Christ came to warn the world of His second coming and the end of the age.

When we consider the multiple reasons that Christ came into the world, we find that He came to serve God, to provide for our salvation, to fulfill the Scriptures, and to transform this world into the Kingdom of God.

However, the truth expressed in I Corinthians 15:3-4 remains always that of first importance.

For what I [Paul] received I passed on to you as of first importance: that Christ died for our sins according to the Scriptures, that he was buried, that he was raised on the third day according to the Scriptures. (1 Cor 15:3-4)

And so we conclude with glorifying and praising God for the Incarnation of His Son.

Bibliography

Brown, Colin, ed., *The New International Dictionary of New Testament Theology,* Grand Rapids, Michigan, Zondervan, 1971

Bruce, F.F. *Paul, the Apostle of the Heart set Free,* Grand Rapids, Michigan, William B. Erdman, 1977

Bullinger, E.W. *A Critical Lexicon and Concordance to the English and Greek New Testament,* Grand Rapids, Michigan, Zondervan 1975

Elwell, Walter, ed., *Topical Analysis of the Bible,* Grand Rapids, Michigan: Baker House Books, 1972

Miller, M.S, and J.L., *Harper's Bible Dictionary*, New York, Harper and Brothers, 1951

PC Study Bible formatted electronic database, Copyright 2003 Biblesoft Inc

Stott, John R.W., *Understanding the Bible*, Grand Rapids, Michigan, Zondervan, 1982

Stott, John R.W., *The Cross of Christ,* Intervarsity Press, 1986

Wetmore, William H. *You Must be Born Again.* Enumclaw, Washington: Winepress Publishing 2003

Wetmore, William H. *Him We Proclaim.* Enumclaw, Washington, Winepress Publishing 2002